COOKING IN NEW ENGLAND

Indigenous Indian tribes lived in the northeastern region of the "new world" for thousands of years until 1620 when English Pilgrims arrived to establish a home where they could practice religious freedom. New England was the first of the North American British colonies to demonstrate ambitions of political freedom that culminated in the War of Independence (1775-1783). Upon the successful conclusion of the war, New England colonies formally united as states in a union called the United States of America.

Little could the Puritans imagine what they had started at their little colony in Plymouth. However, William Bradford, governor of the colony in 1630, glimpsed a vision when he wrote: "Thus out of small beginnings greater things have been produced by His hand that made all things of nothing, and gives being to all things that are; and, as one small candle may light a thousand, so the light here kindled hath shone unto many, yea in some sort to our whole nation."

New England's cuisine developed from the land, the sea and the people. Early explorers returned to England with reports of a "vast sea covered with fish"… fish so plentiful that they could be caught simply by lowering a bucket into the water. Although not as numerous now as in the past, populations of cod, haddock, striped bass, bluefish, flounder and shellfish live in the regional waters. Ironically, lobsters were so abundant that they were known as a poor man's supper while today, lobster is a high-priced treat for the wealthy.

Blueberries, cranberries and concord grapes are native New England plants. Maple syrup is a major food product harvested from the sap of sweet maple and black maple trees that grow in northeastern states. Potatoes are the most widely-grown vegetable crop while apples are the most valuable fruit crop. Other local produce includes peas, beans, corn, eggplant, squashes, onions and beets. Traditional New England cooking has changed little over the years and is popular throughout the country. Beef and pork, slaughtered in the fall and preserved with salt, provided boiled dinners throughout the winter. Today, New England boiled dinner is still a classic favorite. Flavors are sweet or salty. Salt pork and bacon are used for frying; maple syrup, molasses and honey are used for sweetening. Spices and herbs from kitchen gardens add variety. Corn for bread and pudding, eggs, milk, cheese and butter produced on local dairy farms, as well as seasonal vegetables, all contribute to a nourishing, soul-satisfying New England cuisine.

Historians report that Indians probably lived in the Massachusetts region more than 3,000 years ago. Early white explorers first saw Algonquian Indians in the area about 1500. By the time the Pilgrims arrived in 1620, the Indian population had dropped from about 30,000 to about 7,000 because of disease. The Pilgrims almost did not survive their first winter in the new land. They had little food, except the game they could hunt, and their houses were crude bark shelters. About half of the settlers died. Early in 1621, the survivors became friendly with some Indians who taught them to plant corn and beans. By the time cold weather set in again, the settlers were living more comfortably. They had enough food to last through the winter and celebrated the first New England thanksgiving that winter year.

The settlers thanked God for their blessings and celebrated with a harvest festival that lasted three days. The menu included clams, eel and other fish, wild plums, leeks and watercress. The men shot ducks, geese and turkeys. Indian guests contributed "five deer". The women made cornbread and pudding and cooked everything over outdoor fires. The custom of Thanksgiving continues to the present as a legal holiday on the fourth Thursday of November.

Today, for most Americans, a "traditional" Thanksgiving meal includes a turkey, with stuffing, cranberry sauce, potatoes, pumpkin pie or sweet potato pie. Cranberries were probably not included in the first harvest dinner and were not mentioned in New England writings until 50 years later when an Englishman wrote about boiling the berries with sugar to make a sauce. Sugar would not have been available in 1621. Likewise, potatoes, that originated in South America, and sweet potatoes, from the Caribbean, had not yet come to North America.

The Pilgrims suffered dreadful hardships and could scarcely have dreamed that their little Plymouth colony was the start of one of the nation's most historic and influential states. The American Revolution began in Massachusetts and much of the early fighting took place there. When the war concluded, Massachusetts became the sixth state and began a long history of growth and prosperity. Presently, the state ranks among the leading commercial fishing states. Service industries and manufacturing are the principal contributors to the economy. Tourism thrives around the Boston area, Cape Cod and neighboring islands, and the Berkshires.

Boston is the capital of Massachusetts and New England's largest city. It is also New England's leading business, financial, educational, medical and transportation center. For over two hundred years, almost the entire population of Boston were English Puritans and their descendants. In the mid 19th century, wave upon wave of European immigrants poured into the city. People of Irish ancestry make up about 15% of the population and Italian ancestry accounts for 10%. After the Civil War and World War I, African Americans flooded into Boston from the Southern States to seek work. These and other ethnic groups contributed their favorite foods and recipes to the melting pot and Boston has become a great food city. The most representative foods are cranberries, cod, corn muffins, wild turkey, navy beans, Boston Cream Pie, Boston Brown Bread, Boston Baked Beans, chocolate chip cookies, the Boston cream doughnut and Parker House rolls.

Pumpkin Pie

1 1/4	cups pumpkin puree
3/4	cup sugar
1/2	teaspoon salt
1/4	teaspoon ground ginger
1	teaspoon ground cinnamon
1	teaspoon flour
2	eggs, lightly beaten
1	cup evaporated milk
2	tablespoons water
1/2	teaspoon vanilla extract
	1 unbaked 9-inch pastry shell

Preheat oven to 400°. Combine pumpkin, sugar, salt, spices and flour in a medium-sized mixing bowl. Add eggs and mix well. Add evaporated milk, water and vanilla. Mix well. Pour into pastry-lined pie pan. Bake at 400° for 15 minutes, reduce heat to 350° and bake 35 minutes longer or until center is set. Serves 6.

AUTUMN SALAD

Dressing:

3	tablespoons cider vinegar
1/4	cup fresh cranberries
3	tablespoons vegetable oil
2	teaspoons sugar
1/8	teaspoon each salt and pepper

Combine the vinegar and cranberries in a saucepan and cook until cranberries are soft. Remove from heat and add the oil, sugar, salt and pepper. Refrigerate until chilled.

2	heads romaine lettuce, washed and dried and torn into bite-size pieces.
2	Anjou pears, sliced
1/2	cup toasted pecans
1/2	cup good quality blue cheese

Arrange the lettuce on 4 salad plates. Top with the sliced pears, toasted pecans and blue cheese. Drizzle over the chilled cranberry dressing. Serve immediately. Serves 4.

● ● ● ● ● ● ● ● ● ● ● ● ● ● ●

LOBSTER BISQUE

2	pounds cooked lobster
1	cup cold water
1	cup clam juice
1/4	cup butter
1/4	cup flour
4	cups milk, scalded
1 1/2	teaspoons salt

Remove meat from cooked lobster shell. Add cold water and clam juice to body bones and tough end of claws, cut into pieces. Bring to a boil and simmer 20 minutes. Drain, reserve liquid and thicken with the flour and butter mixed together. Add the milk that has been scalded. Add the lobster meat, cut into small bite-size pieces. Season to taste. Serves 6-8.

● ● ● ● ● ● ● ● ● ● ● ● ● ● ●

BOSTON BAKED BEANS

1	pound navy beans
1	large onion, chopped
2	tablespoons Dijon mustard
1/2	cup brown sugar
1/4	cup molasses
1	teaspoon salt

In a large bowl, cover the beans with water and soak overnight. Drain the beans and cover with fresh cold water. Cook for 30-40 minutes until beans are tender. Drain. Reserve liquid. Preheat oven to 325°. In a bean or deep casserole with a lid, combine the beans, onion, mustard, sugar, molasses and salt. Add enough of the cooking liquid to just cover the beans. Bake for 2-3 hours, checking frequently to make sure beans are not dry. Add more of reserved cooking liquid if necessary. Uncover the last 20 minutes to make a crusty top. Serves 6-8.

PORTUGUESE FISH SOUP

10-12	medium shell-on shrimp
1	teaspoon salt
1/2	cup chopped parsley
2	tablespoons olive oil
1	large onion, thinly sliced
1	teaspoon chopped garlic
1	pound flaky white fish such as cod or haddock
2-3	cups tomato juice
1/2	cup small pasta, such as orzo.
3	tablespoons chopped fresh cilantro
	Pepper to taste

Bring 3 cups of water to a boil in a medium saucepan. Drop in shrimp and cook for 1-2 minutes until pink. Reserve the cooking liquid. Remove shrimp and drop into cold water to stop the cooking. Peel and return the shells to the reserved cooking liquid. Add the salt and parsley and cook 10-15 minutes.

In another pan, heat the olive oil and sauté the onion and garlic until soft. Cut the fish in bite size pieces and add to pan. Strain the liquid from the shrimp shell mixture. Discard the shells. Add the liquid to pan along with the tomato juice. Add the pasta and half the cilantro and stir briskly. Cook for 6-8 minutes until pasta is cooked. Season to taste. Cut the shrimp into 1/2 inch pieces and add to soup along with the remaining cilantro. Heat through. To serve, put bread cubes (Italian or French) in bottom of soup bowls and ladle soup on top. Serve with extra bread on the side. Serves 6.

● ● ● ● ● ● ● ● ● ● ● ● ● ● ●

NO BAKE COOKIES

2	cups white sugar
1/2	cup butter
1/2	cup milk

Boil above 3 ingredients for 2 minutes. Remove from heat and quickly add:

1/2	cup peanut butter
2	cups quick cooking oats
1/2	cup chocolate syrup
1	teaspoon vanilla

Blend well and drop by teaspoonfuls onto waxed paper.

Paella

1/4	cup olive oil
4	minced garlic cloves
1	large onion, chopped
1	large red pepper, sliced
1 1/2	cups chopped tomatoes
1	pound chorizos, sliced
2	cups raw, shelled shrimp
2	tablespoons capers
1/3	cup tomato paste
12	cherrystone clams
1 1/2	cups bay scallops
1	lobster tail, split in half
1	cup drained fresh oysters
7-8	cups chicken broth
2 1/2	cups long grain rice
2	bay leaves
1	teaspoon oregano
1/2	teaspoon saffron threads
	Tabasco to taste
5	cups cooked, cubed chicken
	Garnishes of cooked peas, olives, pimientos

Heat the olive oil in a paella pan or a wide, shallow, heatproof skillet. [A really big frying pan works too.] When it is very hot, add garlic and cook until it is golden brown. Discard the garlic. Add chopped onions and pepper, and cook about three minutes. Add tomatoes, and cook, stirring for about 5 minutes. Add chorizos, and cook for about 1 minute.

Add the raw shelled shrimp and cook until they turn bright red. Add capers and tomato paste. Stir briefly, and add clams, bay scallops, lobster and drained oysters. Cook, stirring for about 2 minutes. Add 5 cups of chicken broth, bay leaves, oregano and saffron. Gradually sprinkle 2 1/2 cups long grain rice into the pan so that it is evenly distributed. After the rice is added, the paella must be stirred constantly until the dish is finished.

Add Tabasco to taste. After the rice has been cooking for 8-10 minutes, add 2 more cups of hot chicken broth and continue stirring. Cook for about 5 more minutes. Add chicken [the one you used to make the broth], and push it into the stew. Continue cooking and stirring, adding more hot broth as the rice becomes dry. Paella is done when the rice is tender, but it should not be soupy. Remove the bay leaves and garnish with peas, olives, and pimentos. Serves 12-18.

PARKER HOUSE ROLLS

Parker House rolls are said to have originated during the 1870s at Boston's Parker House Hotel that opened in 1856. They are made by folding a butter-brushed round of dough in half, leaving a creased center and an abundance of crusty surface when baked. The outside is crisp and the inside is soft.

| 1 | package (2 1/4 teaspoons) active dry yeast |
| 3 | tablespoons warm water |

Add:

1	cup whole or low-fat milk, warmed to 105-115°
5	tablespoons melted butter
3	tablespoons sugar
1	large egg
1	teaspoon salt

Mix 1 minute by hand.
Gradually stir in:

| 2 | cups bread flour |

Then add:

| 1 1/2 | cups more bread flour |

Knead about 10 minutes by hand or with dough hook. Transfer to oiled bowl. Cover loosely with plastic wrap. Let rise until doubled in volume, 1 to 1 1/2 hours. Punch the dough down, knead briefly, and refrigerate, covered, for 30 minutes.

Divide dough into 18 pieces about 1 ounce each. Roll dough pieces into balls, loosely cover with oiled plastic wrap, and let rest 10 minutes. Grease a baking sheet. With a rolling pin or a dowel, roll just the center of each round to create an oval. Edges should be slightly thicker than the center. Brush tops lightly with melted butter and fold the ovals in half so the two ends meet. Let rise until doubled in volume, about 1 hour. Preheat oven to 425 degrees. Brush tops with melted butter. Bake until golden brown, about 15 minutes. Makes 18 rolls.

COD FISH CAKES

1	pound salt cod
4	large potatoes, peeled and chopped
3	eggs
1/2	cup finely chopped parsley
1	tablespoon finely diced onion
1/2	teaspoon freshly ground black pepper
	Vegetable oil

Soak codfish in cold water overnight. Next day, pour off water and add enough fresh water to cover the fish. Bring to a boil. If the water and fish are still salty, drain and add fresh water again and bring to a boil. In the meantime, cook the potatoes until tender. Mash the cod (drained) and potatoes (drained) together. Add the onion, parsley, eggs and pepper and mix well. Shape into balls and flatten into patty shape. Heat oil in a large skillet and fry patties until browned on both sides. Drain on paper towels. Serves 4-6.

HARVARD BEETS

3/4	cup white sugar
4	teaspoons cornstarch
1/2	cup white vinegar
1/3	cup water
2	15-ounce cans sliced beets, drained
3	tablespoons butter
1/4	teaspoon salt
1/4	teaspoon pepper

Combine the sugar, cornstarch, vinegar and water in a saucepan. Bring to a boil and cook for 4-5 minutes. Add the beets to the liquid and simmer for 30 minutes over low heat. Stir in the butter and seasonings. Serve warm or chilled.

Acorn Street

Boston Italian Style Pizza

1	purchased fresh pizza dough
1/2	cup olive oil, preferably extra-virgin
1	cup tomato sauce
3	cups (about 12 oz.) shredded Mozzarella cheese
3	garlic cloves, minced or pressed

Toppings, choose 1 or a combination: cooked & crumbled sweet Italian sausage, anchovy fillets, sautéed sliced fresh mushrooms, sliced pepperoni, sliced cooked Italian meatballs, sliced green or red sweet pepper, sliced red or yellow sweet onion, ripe olives, crushed dried red chili pepper (all optional)

1 1/2	teaspoon dried oregano
1/3	cup (about 1 1/2 oz.) freshly grated Parmesan cheese

Cornmeal, if using a pizza peel
Pizza stone for oven

Prepare the dough and preheat the oven to 425°. Place the pizza stone in the middle oven rack. Roll out or stretch the pizza dough and place the dough on a pizza peel generously sprinkled with cornmeal or on a lightly oiled pizza screen. Brush dough all over with the best quality extra virgin olive oil, and then add the Mozzarella cheese, leaving a 1/2 inch border around the edges. Top with the garlic and cover with the tomato sauce. Put the tomato sauce over the Mozzarella to get a good crust. Add 1 or more of the toppings, if desired, and sprinkle with the oregano and the fresh grated Parmesan cheese. Drizzle evenly with olive oil. Transfer the pizza to the pizza stone in the preheated oven and bake until the crust is golden brown and puffy, about 10-15 minutes. Remove from the oven to a cutting tray or board and lightly brush the crust with olive oil. Slice and serve immediately.

Whole Grain Pancakes

1	cup whole wheat flour
3	tablespoons all-purpose flour
4	tablespoons uncooked Cream of Wheat
3	tablespoons sugar
1	teaspoon baking soda
1	teaspoon baking powder
1/2	teaspoon salt
1-1 1/2	cups buttermilk (enough to make a medium-thick batter)
2	tablespoons melted butter
1	large beaten egg
	Raisins, walnuts

Combine flours, cream of wheat, sugar, baking soda, baking powder and salt. Combine the buttermilk, butter and egg and add to dry ingredients. Ladle batter (about 1/4 cup per pancake). Sprinkle top with a few raisins and walnuts. When top side has bubbles, gently turn and cook another minute. Serve with maple syrup and butter. Serves 4.

• • • • • • • • • • • • • • • • • • • •

Linguine with Seafood

1/4	cup olive oil
1/4	cup butter
1	large onion, chopped
3	garlic cloves, minced
1/2	teaspoon dried rosemary
1/2	cup dried oregano
1	28-ounce can tomatoes, chopped
	Salt and pepper to taste
1	cup dry white wine
1/2	cup chopped parsley
1	pound linguine, cooked according to package directions
	Combination of shrimp, lobster, crab, scallops, cod

In a large skillet, heat the butter and oil, sauté the onion until translucent. Add the garlic and cook 1 more minute. Add the wine and continue cooking until liquid evaporates. Lower heat and add the tomatoes, spices, salt and pepper to taste. Add the seafood and cook another 5-7 minutes until fish is cooked. Serve over hot cooked linguine. Serves 4-6.

Boston Brown Bread

This is the traditional accompaniment to baked beans.

1	cup rye flour
1	cup yellow cornmeal
1	cup white flour
2	teaspoons baking soda
1	teaspoon salt
3/4	cup molasses
2	cups buttermilk

Mix dry ingredients; stir in molasses and buttermilk, mixing well, but do not beat. Fill 1-1/2 quart mold two-thirds full. Cover with tight-fitting lid or aluminum foil. Place on a rack in a tightly covered Dutch oven or stock pot; containing a small amount of boiling water. Steam 2 to 3-1/2 hours, or until wooden pick inserted in center comes out clean. Keep water boiling over low heat throughout cooking, adding more water as needed. (To add, boil water in another container, lift lid and quickly add water so that the least possible amount of steam is lost). Remove from mold and serve hot with butter (or remove and wrap in waxed paper and return to mold to reheat later). Makes enough for one 7-inch tube mold or four 1-pound cans. Serves 8 to 10.

• • • • • • • • • • • • • • • • • • • •

Irish Soda Bread

4	cups flour
1	teaspoon salt
8	teaspoons baking powder
1/4	cup sugar
2	eggs plus enough buttermilk to make two cups
1	cup raisins

Preheat oven to 350°. Sift dry ingredients into a bowl. Add raisins. Beat eggs in a 2 cup measure and add buttermilk to equal 2 cups. Pour milk and eggs over dry ingredients. Mix until blended. Turn out onto a floured board and knead a couple of times. Shape into a round loaf. Place in a 9-inch greased cast iron skillet. Make an X with a sharp knife across the top of the dough. Bake in preheated oven for 60 minutes. Remove from pan and cool completely.

Boston Common, America's oldest public park

Curried Pumpkin Soup

2	medium onions, finely chopped (2 cups)
2	tablespoons unsalted butter
1	large garlic clove, minced
2	tablespoons curry powder
1 1/2	teaspoons salt
1/2	teaspoon dried hot red pepper flakes
2	(15-oz) cans solid-pack pumpkin (not pie filling)
4	cups water
1 1/2	cups reduced-sodium chicken broth
1	can unsweetened coconut milk (not low-fat)

Cook onions in butter in a wide 6-quart heavy pot over moderately low heat, stirring occasionally, until softened, 3 to 5 minutes. Add garlic and curry powder, stirring, 1 minute. Stir in salt, red pepper flakes, pumpkin, water, broth, and coconut milk and simmer, uncovered, stirring occasionally, 30 minutes. Purée soup in batches in a blender until smooth (use caution when blending hot liquids). Transfer to a large bowl, and return soup to pot. Keep soup warm over low heat Serves 6.

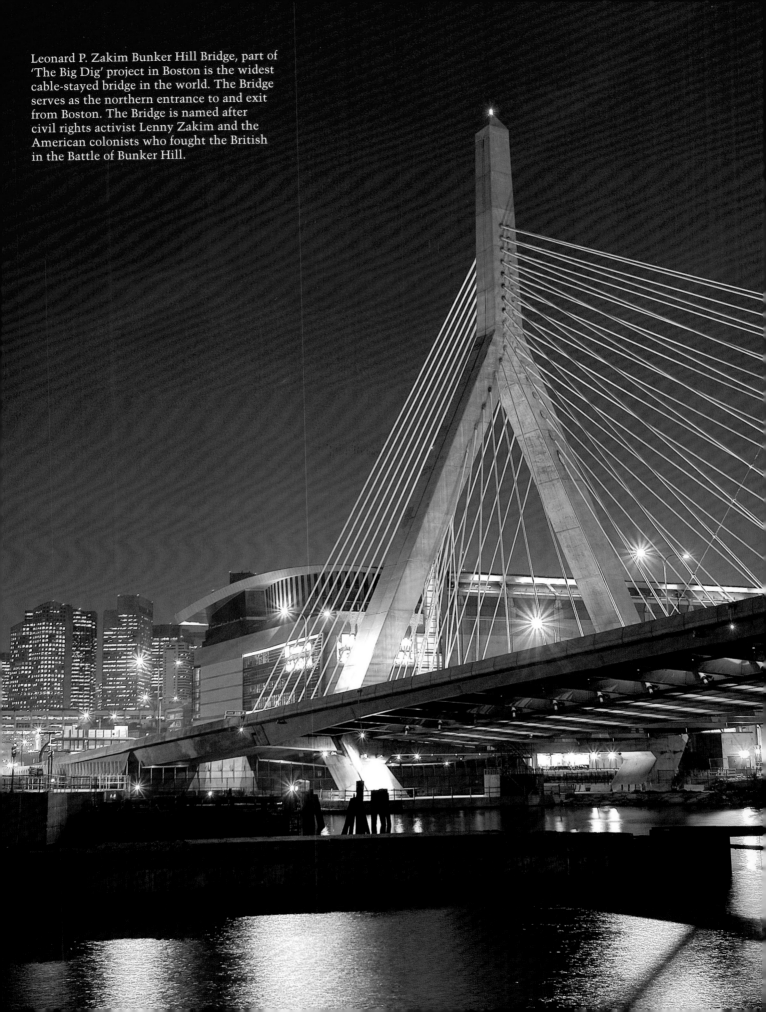

Leonard P. Zakim Bunker Hill Bridge, part of
'The Big Dig' project in Boston is the widest
cable-stayed bridge in the world. The Bridge
serves as the northern entrance to and exit
from Boston. The Bridge is named after
civil rights activist Lenny Zakim and the
American colonists who fought the British
in the Battle of Bunker Hill.

In a park in central Boston is an endearing sculpture in honor of the time-honored children's classic, _Make Way for Ducklings_, by Robert McCloskey. First printed in 1941, it is as popular today as it was over 60 years ago. It tells the story of a pair of Mallard ducks that decided to raise their family on a little island in the lagoon in Boston Public Garden.

Boston Cream Doughnuts

Dough:

1/4	cup warm water
2	tablespoons instant yeast
1	cup warm milk
1/4	cup vegetable shortening
2	eggs
1/4	cup sugar
1	teaspoon salt
3 1/2-4	cups all-purpose flour

Custard Filling:

1/4	cup sugar
3	tablespoons all-purpose flour
3	egg yolks
1	cup milk, plus
2	tablespoons milk
1	tablespoon unsalted butter
1/2	teaspoon pure vanilla extract

Chocolate Glaze:

1	tablespoon unsalted butter
2	ounces semisweet chocolate, chopped
1 1/2	cups icing sugar
1/2	teaspoon pure vanilla extract
1/3	cup hot water

For the dough, place the water and yeast together in the bowl of an electric mixer and let stand for 2 to 3 minutes to dissolve the yeast. Mix in the milk and shortening. Stir in the eggs, sugar, salt and 3 cups of the flour. Mix to make a soft dough. Knead with the dough hook on the lowest speed of the mixer for 8 to 10 minutes, gradually adding more flour as required to form a soft but elastic dough. Place the dough in a lightly greased bowl; cover the bowl with a damp cloth and let rise for 45 minutes or until doubled.

For the filling, whisk the sugar, flour, and egg yolks together in a bowl. In a small saucepan, bring the milk to a boil. Stir 2 tablespoons of the hot milk into the egg yolk mixture to temper the yolks and prevent curdling. Stir the egg mixture into the milk and stir constantly until thickened and beginning to boil gently. Remove from heat. Stir in the butter and vanilla and let cool. Place in a bowl, covering with plastic wrap to help prevent a skin from forming. Put in the fridge until needed. Turn the dough onto a lightly floured surface. Pinch off pieces and form into small balls, about the size of golf balls. Cover and let rise for 25 minutes.

In a Dutch oven heat 4 inches of oil to 375*F. Fry a few at a time to a golden brown on first side. Turn and fry on the second side for 15 to 30 seconds. Using a slotted spoon, transfer to paper towels to drain and let cool. Whisk the custard to smooth and fluff it. Put the custard in a pastry bag fitted with a large plain tip. Make a small hole in each cooled doughnut and pipe in some custard. For the glaze, melt the butter and chocolate in a double boiler over barely simmering water. Add the sugar and vanilla, stirring until smooth. Add enough water to make a thin glaze. Let cool for 1 minute, and then drizzle over the doughnuts. If the glaze gets too stiff, add more hot water to make it workable again.

Gingerbread

1	cup sifted flour
1	teaspoon baking soda
1/4	teaspoon salt
2	teaspoons cinnamon
1	teaspoon ground ginger
1	egg, lightly beaten
1/3	cup dark brown sugar
1/2	cup dark molasses
1/2	cup buttermilk
1/4	cup butter, melted

Preheat oven to 350°. Sift together the flour, salt, soda and spices. In a mixing bowl, combine beaten egg, sugar, molasses, buttermilk, and melted butter. Add the dry ingredients and mix thoroughly. Turn batter into a greased and floured 9-inch square pan and bake for 25-30 minutes. Serve warm with whipped cream.

Chicken or Turkey Tetrazzini

1/4	cup plus 2 tablespoons butter, softened
1/4	cup flour
1/2	teaspoon salt and pepper
1/2	cup chopped onion
1	stalk celery, chopped
1	cup chicken broth
1/2	cup sour cream
2	tablespoon sherry wine
7	ounces spaghetti (cooked)
2 –3	cups cooked chicken or turkey, cut in bite-size pieces
1	3 - ounce jar mushrooms
1/2	cup grated Parmesan cheese
	Slivered almonds (optional)

Preheat oven to 350°. In a large skillet, sauté the onion and celery in 2 tablespoons butter until translucent. Mix the 1/4 cup butter with the flour and seasonings. Add to the skillet. Cook 1 minute. Stir in broth and sour cream. Cook 1 minute more. Add sherry wine and chicken, almonds, mushrooms. Heat through. Using a 9 x 13-inch casserole dish, layer spaghetti, then sauce. Sprinkle with Parmesan cheese. Bake until hot and bubbling, about 30-40 minutes. Serves 4-6.

Bunker Hill

Oysters on the Half Shell

The qualities of a raw oyster are usually described in terms of three elements: texture, degree of sweetness/salinity, and mineral/marine plant life flavor. Traditionally, oysters are presented six to a plate, arranged on a low serving dish with oysters anchored in Kosher salt. Strategies for adding condiments vary. For some, any addition to the oyster is heresy; for others, a drop of lemon, a little mignonette sauce, a hint of black pepper, or a dab of hot sauce is ideal. Restraint in condiment use is crucial, though, because the flavor of the oyster is easily overwhelmed.

LAMB CHOPS WITH FRESH HERBS

1/3	cup vegetable oil
1/3	cup red wine vinegar
2	tablespoons soy sauce
1	tablespoon lemon juice
1	tablespoon seasoned salt
1/2	teaspoon each: garlic powder, oregano, rosemary, thyme, marjoram, and dry mustard and white pepper
8	lamb loin chops (about 2-1/2 pounds) cut 1-inch thick

Combine all ingredients, except lamb; mix well. Remove 1/2 of marinade for basting. Place chops in a resealable plastic bag and pour remaining marinade over them. Seal bag and refrigerate for at least 1 hour, turning occasionally. Remove chops from marinade. Discard used marinade. Grill or broil chops until desired doneness, about 8 minutes, turning once and basting often with remaining 1/2 marinade. Discard any remaining marinade. Makes 4 to 6 servings.

APPLE PIE

	Pastry for a 2-crust pie
6	cups tart apples, peeled and sliced (Granny Smith works well)
2/3	cup sugar
3	tablespoons flour
1	teaspoon lemon juice
1-2	teaspoons cinnamon
1/4	teaspoon ground nutmeg
2	tablespoons butter

Preheat oven to 375°. Line a 9-inch pie pan with pastry. In a large bowl, mix together the apples, sugar, flour, lemon juice and spices. Mix well. Fill the pie shell with the apple mixture. Dot with butter. Cover with top crust, sealing edges well. Sprinkle with sugar and make several slashes in top crust to vent the steam. Bake approximately 50-60 minutes. Makes 6-8 servings.

Aerial view of Fenway Park, Boston, MA

Steamed Clams with Bacon, Tomato and Spinach

6	slices bacon, chopped
1	small onion, chopped
2	minced large garlic cloves
1/4	teaspoon red pepper flakes
2	pounds ripe fresh tomatoes, chopped
3	dozen small hard-shelled clams, scrubbed clean
4	ounces fresh baby spinach.

Cook bacon in a heavy pot over medium heat until bacon begins to brown. Add the onion, garlic and red pepper flakes until onion is cooked through. Do not allow to brown. Add tomatoes and cook until tomatoes break down and sauce thickens, about 10 minutes. Increase heat and add the clams. Cover pot and cook until clams open, stirring occasionally. After 10 minutes discard any clams that do not open. Stir in the spinach and cook for 1 more minute. Season with salt and pepper if needed. Serve with the sauce and lots of crusty French bread.

CAPE COD

"Cape Cod is the bare and bended arm of Massachusetts" said Henry David Thoreau, one of the state's famous native sons. The 65-mile-long peninsula is half land and half water, partly piney woods and pristine sea shores, sprinkled with quaint villages and weathered cottages and accented by flotillas of colorful pleasure craft and rusty fishing boats. The cape was named for the abundant numbers of codfish living offshore. Cranberries grew wild in the marshes of the Cape's low-lying bogs. When the three-masted galleon, *Mayflower*, arrived at the tip of Cape Cod in 1620 with 102 men, women and children, the tiny band of settlers stayed a month on the Cape before moving to the mainland and settling at Plymouth.

Over the next 25 years, many more colonists from Europe arrived and some settled on the Cape. The newcomers established small farms and raised sheep and cattle however the limited amount of land on the thickly-forested Cape was not very fertile and yielded modest amounts of food. From the beginning, fishing was the principal enterprise. Nearly all the towns founded on the Cape supported large fishing fleets. By the middle 19th century, Provincetown maintained one of the most prosperous fishing fleets in the country with hundreds of vessels and 75 wharves. High quality fish were shipped to Europe in exchange for fruits and wines and traded to the West Indies for molasses and sugar.

Beginning about the turn of the 19th century, visitors discovered the charm of Cape Cod and the hospitality industry grew to dominate the local economy. Today, there are 230,000 year-round residents with an explosion of tourists during the summer.

New England *Clambake*

The traditional New England clambake is a ritual older than New England itself. Native Americans perfected this method of cooking food in a rock-lined sand pit long before the English, French and Spanish explorers touched the beaches of the New World. This important regional feast requires the freshest-possible soft-shell clams and usually includes mussels, Maine lobsters, red potatoes, sweet onion, corn-on-the-cob and plenty of butter for dipping. Follow up with cold watermelon for dessert.

Preparing for a clambake is a day-long project. First, invite your friends to help dig a hole in firm sand, 3-feet deep and 4-to 6-feet across. Line the pit with round or oval dry rocks, about the size of an adult's head. Build a fire in the hole with firewood from home (do not count on finding enough suitable driftwood). Keep the fire burning hot for 4 hours to heat the rocks to high temperature. Test by sprinkling water over rocks. Check all the rocks for even heat. If water sizzles, the rocks are ready. When rocks are white-hot, rake out wood and ashes. Cover the bottom rocks with 3-to 6-inches of wet seaweed to create as much steam as possible. Add a layer of washed, tightly-shut clams, another layer of seaweed; a layer of live lobsters and mussels, more seaweed; a layer of small potatoes and onions, more seaweed; a layer of unhusked corn and a final layer of seaweed. Cover the entire hole with a wet tarpaulin and anchor securely with rocks so that steam cannot escape. Allow to steam for 1 hour or more. Periodically, check by poking a stick through the layers. The clambake is finished when clams are open, lobsters are bright red and the potatoes can be easily pierced with a fork. Serve with melted butter and offer vinegar, Tabasco sauce, Worcestershire sauce and lemon slices on the side.

Chicken Pot Pie

2	sheets Puff Pastry
1	pound boneless, skinless chicken, cut into bite-size pieces
2	cups chicken broth
1	tablespoon vegetable oil
1	medium onion, chopped
3	medium carrots, chopped
2	celery stalks, sliced
	Salt and pepper to taste
3	tablespoons butter
1/3	cup flour
1 1/2	cups milk
1/2	teaspoon poultry seasoning
2	tablespoons dry sherry
1	cup frozen or fresh green peas
1	tablespoon chopped fresh parsley

Thaw puff pastry. Cut out circles large enough to cover serving dishes. Refrigerate. Preheat oven to 400°. In a large saucepan simmer the chicken in the broth for 10-15 minutes. Transfer broth and chicken to separate bowls. Place oil in the saucepan and sauté the vegetables until tender. Season with salt and pepper. Transfer the vegetables to bowl with the reserved chicken. Heat butter in same saucepan. Add flour and cook for 1 minute. Whisk in the reserved broth, milk, and poultry seasoning. Season to taste and add the sherry. Add the vegetables and chicken along with the peas and parsley. Divide mixture among 4-6 ovenproof baking dishes or small casseroles. Top with the pastry rounds. Bake in preheated oven for 30-40 minutes or until bubbly and the pastry is browned. Serves 4-6.

● ● ● ● ● ● ● ● ● ● ● ● ● ● ● ● ●

Chicken Noodle Soup

1	3-pound broiler/fryer chicken
1-1/2	teaspoons salt
	Water to cover chicken
1-1/2	cups fine noodles
1	small onion, chopped
1	carrot, pared and diced
1	celery stalk, thinly sliced
1	bay leaf
	Additional salt and pepper to taste

Wash chicken, remove innards but do not cut up. Cover chicken with water in large pot. Add salt. Heat to boiling. Reduce heat; cover and simmer 1-1/2 hours or until chicken is tender.

Remove chicken from broth. Remove meat from bones and cut into small pieces. Skim fat from broth. Measure broth into medium saucepan (add water if necessary to have 5 cups). Add chicken meat and remaining ingredients. Heat to boiling. Reduce heat and simmer until noodles are tender, about 15 minutes. Remove bay leaf before serving. Makes 6 servings.

Holiday Roast Turkey with Sage Onion Stuffing

1	15-18 pound fresh or frozen and thawed turkey

Stuffing:

1/2	cup butter
1	cup chopped onion
1	cup chopped celery
1	medium apple, peeled and chopped
1	package boxed herb stuffing mix
1	tablespoon dried sage
3	tablespoons chopped fresh parsley
	Salt and Pepper to taste

Sauté the onion, celery and apple in the butter until vegetables are cooked. Follow the package directions for the stuffing, add the sautéed vegetables, sage and parsley. Season with salt and pepper. Toss lightly. Fill cavity of turkey with the stuffing. Do not pack too tightly. Put leftover stuffing in a buttered casserole, cover with foil or lid, and bake along with turkey during last hour of baking. Bake turkey at 325° for 20 minutes per pound. Tent with foil if turkey browns too fast. Let rest 15 minutes before carving.

● ● ● ● ● ● ● ● ● ● ● ● ● ● ● ● ●

Parmesan Baked Potatoes

3	tablespoons butter
2	tablespoons grated Parmesan cheese
4	medium unpeeled Red Bliss potatoes, halved
1	tablespoon butter (additional)

Preheat oven to 400°. Pour butter into a small baking dish. Sprinkle in the cheese. Place the potatoes into the butter and cheese cut side down. Drizzle the 1 tablespoon butter over the tops of potatoes. Bake uncovered for 45-50 minutes or until potatoes are tender and browned. Serves 3-4.

Aerial view of Provincetown

New England Boiled Dinner

4-5	pounds corned beef
6	small onions, peeled
6	small turnips, peeled
8	small potatoes
6	medium carrots, peeled
1	small head cabbage, cut into eighths

In a large soup pot, add the corned beef and enough cold water to completely cover the beef. Bring to a simmer and cook 3 hours. Add the onions and turnips. 30 minutes later add the potatoes and carrots. After another 15 minutes, add the cabbage. Cook another 7-10 minutes. To serve, remove beef and vegetables to a platter. Mustard and horseradish are traditional accompaniments.

CRANBERRY MEATBALLS

2	eggs, beaten
1	cup cornflake crumbs
1/3	cup ketchup
2	tablespoons light soy sauce
1	tablespoon dried parsley
2	tablespoons dried minced onion
1/2	teaspoon salt
1/4	teaspoon pepper
3	pounds ground pork

Sauce:

1	can jellied cranberry sauce
1	cup ketchup
3	tablespoons brown sugar
1	tablespoon lemon juice

Preheat oven to 350°. In a mixing bowl, combine the first eight ingredients. Add the pork and mix well. Shape into 1-inch meatballs. Place in a 13 x 9 inch baking pan. Bake for 20-30 minutes. Remove from oven and remove meatballs to paper towels to drain. In a large saucepan combine the sauce ingredients. Cook, stirring constantly, until cranberry sauce is melted. Add the meatballs and simmer 3-4 minutes. Serve hot. Makes about 60.

● ● ● ● ● ● ● ● ● ● ● ● ● ●

FISH WITH SPINACH AND CHEESE

2	tablespoons butter
2	tablespoons flour
1	teaspoon instant chicken bouillon
	Dash of black pepper, nutmeg, and red pepper
1	cup milk
3/4	cup shredded Swiss cheese
1	package (10 ounces) frozen chopped spinach, thawed and well drained
1	tablespoon lemon juice
1	pound cod fish fillets, cut into serving size pieces
	Salt to taste
3	tablespoons grated Parmesan cheese
	Paprika for garnish

Preheat oven to 350°. Melt butter in a saucepan over low heat. Stir in the flour, bouillon, peppers and nutmeg. Cook over low heat, stirring constantly for 1-2 minutes. Add the milk. Stirring constantly, cook another minute. Add the cheese and stir just until cheese melts. Remove from heat and set aside. Place spinach in an 8 or 9-inch casserole dish. Sprinkle with the lemon juice. Arrange the fish pieces on top. Spread sauce over the top. Bake uncovered in a preheated oven until fish is flaky, about 20-25 minutes. Sprinkle with the Parmesan cheese and paprika and bake an additional 5-7 minutes. Serves 4.

CHICKEN DIVAN

2	packages (10 ounces each) frozen broccoli or 1 1/2 pounds fresh broccoli florets.
1 1/2	cups cooked chicken, cut into bite-size pieces

Sauce:

1	can Cream of Chicken soup, undiluted
1/2	cup mayonnaise
2	tablespoons fresh lemon juice
2	tablespoons sherry
1/4	cup grated Parmesan cheese

Preheat oven to 350°. If using fresh broccoli, steam until partially cooked. Arrange broccoli in bottom of a greased 1-quart casserole dish. Add the chicken pieces to the top. Combine all the sauce ingredients and spoon over the top of broccoli and chicken. Bake uncovered for 30-40 minutes. Dish should be bubbly and lightly browned on top. Serves 4.

● ● ● ● ● ● ● ● ● ● ● ● ● ● ● ●

WORLD'S BEST SUGAR COOKIES

1	cup butter
1	cup confectioner's sugar
1	cup granulated sugar
2	eggs
1	cup vegetable oil
2	teaspoons vanilla
1	teaspoon baking soda
1	teaspoon cream of tartar
1/2	teaspoon salt
5	cups flour
	Granulated sugar for dipping

Preheat oven to 350°. In a medium bowl, cream butter with confectioner's sugar and granulated sugar. Beat in eggs until smooth. Slowly add in oil, vanilla, baking soda, cream of tartar, salt and flour. Chill dough for easy handling. Shape into walnut-size balls. Dip in sugar. Place on a baking sheet and press down. Bake in preheated oven 10-12 minutes or until lightly brown. Do not overbake. Makes about 4 dozen cookies.

Cranberry Harvest, Cape Cod, MA

Cranberry Nut Bread

	Juice and grated peel of 1 orange
	Boiling water
2	tablespoons butter
1	cup sugar
1	egg
1	cup chopped fresh cranberries
1/2	cup chopped walnuts
2	cups flour
1/2	teaspoon salt
1/2	teaspoon baking soda
1/2	teaspoon baking powder

Preheat oven to 325°. Put orange juice in a 1 cup measure. Add enough boiling water to make 3/4 cup. Add the grated peel and butter. Stir until butter is melted. Set aside. In a mixing bowl, beat sugar and egg together; add the orange mixture and stir until well blended. Add the cranberries and nuts. Sift together the flour, salt, baking soda, and baking powder. Stir into the egg mixture. Pour into a greased 9"x5"x3" loaf pan. Bake in preheated oven for about 1 hour or until a toothpick inserted in center comes out clean. Cool and store overnight before serving.

SALMON LOAF

2   cans (14-ounce) salmon, drained and liquid reserved
2   large eggs
1   cup milk, approximately
3   cups coarse soda cracker crumbs
1/4   cup chopped green onions
2   tablespoons lemon juice
2   tablespoons chopped fresh parsley
1/4   teaspoon salt
1/4   teaspoon pepper
    Lemon slices for garnish

Preheat oven to 350°. Grease a loaf pan 9" x 5" x 3". In a large bowl, mix the salmon and eggs. Add enough milk to the reserved salmon liquid to make 1 1/2 cups. Stir in liquid and remaining ingredients, except lemon. Spoon lightly into prepared pan. Bake about 45 minutes or until center is set. Garnish with the lemon and more parsley. Serve hot. Serves 6-8.

BLUEBERRY STRUESEL MUFFINS

1   cup milk
1/4   cup vegetable oil
1/2   teaspoon vanilla
1   large egg
2   cups all-purpose flour
1/3   cup sugar
3   teaspoons baking powder
1/2   teaspoon salt
1   cup fresh or canned (drained) blueberries

Topping:
2   tablespoons butter
1/4   cup all-purpose flour
2   tablespoons packed brown sugar
1/4   teaspoon ground cinnamon

Preheat oven to 400°. Grease bottoms of 12 muffin cups or use paper cup liners. Prepare the topping by thoroughly blending the 4 ingredients in a small bowl. Set aside. Beat the milk, oil, vanilla and egg in a bowl. Add the dry ingredients until flour is just moistened. Fold in the blueberries. Divide the batter among the 12 muffin cups. Sprinkle each with about 2 teaspoons topping. Bake for 20-25 minutes in preheated oven. Immediately remove from muffin tins and cool on a rack. Serve warm.

Brandt Point Light, Cape Cod, MA

Poached Salmon with Lemon-Dill Sauce

1	teaspoon olive or vegetable oil
2	tablespoon finely chopped shallots
1 1/2	cups lowfat milk
1/2	teaspoon salt
	Freshly ground black pepper to taste
1 1/2	pounds salmon fillet, about 1 inch thick, skin on, cut into 4 portions

Lemon Dill Sauce

1	cup mayonnaise
1	cup sour cream
2	tablespoons fresh dill, finely chopped
1	tablespoon lemon juice

Whip with whisk until almost pouring consistency. Store in refrigerator.

In a 10-inch skillet or sauté pan, heat oil over medium heat. Add shallots and sauté until softened, 30 to 60 seconds. Add milk, salt and pepper; bring to simmer, stirring. Reduce heat to low. Slip in salmon pieces, skin-side up; immediately turn over. Cover and poach gently, spooning cooking liquid over top of salmon occasionally, just until interior is opaque, 10 to 12 minutes. With a slotted spoon, carefully transfer salmon to a warm platter. Cover and keep warm. Serve cold or warm with the lemon dill sauce. Makes 4 servings.

Twenty-Four Hour Fruit Salad

1	can (16 1/2 ounces) pitted light or dark cherries, drained well
2	cans (15-ounce each)) pineapple chunks, drained with 2 tablespoons juice reserved
3	oranges, cut into small chunks or 2 cans mandarin oranges, drained
1 1/2	cups miniature marshmallows

Prepare the Dressing:

2	large eggs, beaten
2	tablespoons sugar
2	tablespoons lemon juice
2	tablespoons reserved pineapple juice
1	tablespoon butter
	Dash of salt
3/4	cup heavy whipping cream

Heat all ingredients except the cream just to boiling in a saucepan over medium heat, stirring constantly. Cool. Beat whipping cream in chilled bowl until stiff peaks form. Fold in cooled egg mixture.

In a large glass bowl (a trifle bowl is nice) gently toss the fruit, marshmallows and dressing. Cover and refrigerate at least 12 hours but no more than 24 hours. Serves 8-10.

Veal Parmigiana

2	cups tomato sauce
1	large egg
1/4	cup mayonnaise
3/4	cup dry breadcrumbs
1/2	cup grated Parmesan cheese
1 1/2	pounds veal cutlets for the scaloppini
1/4	cup olive oil
2	cups shredded Mozzarella cheese

Preheat oven to 350°. Mix the egg and mayonnaise in a flat dish. Mix the breadcrumbs and grated Parmesan cheese in another flat dish. Make the scaloppini by cutting the veal into 2 pieces and place each between 2 sheets of waxed paper. Pound until about 1/4 inch thickness. Heat the oil in a 12-inch skillet over medium high heat. Dip the scaloppini in the egg mixture and then in the crumbs. Fry in hot fat until browned on both sides (Do not fry too many at one time). Drain on paper towels and brown remaining scaloppini. In a medium baking dish, put one layer of scaloppini. Spoon over 1/2 the sauce, sprinkle 1 cup of Mozzarella over the sauce. Repeat this layer. Bake uncovered about 30 minutes or until sauce is bubbly and cheese is lightly browned. Serves 4-6.

Russian Tea Cakes

1	cup butter, softened
1/2	cup powdered sugar
1	teaspoon vanilla
2 1/4	cups all-purpose flour
3/4	cup finely chopped nuts
1/4	teaspoon salt
	Powdered sugar

Preheat oven to 400°. Mix the butter, 1/2 cup powdered sugar and the vanilla in a large bowl. Stir in the flour, nuts and salt until dough holds together. Shape into 1-inch balls. Place about 1 inch apart on ungreased cookie sheet. Bake 10-12 minutes or until set but not brown. Remove from cookie sheet. Cool slightly. Roll warm cookies in powdered sugar. Cool completely on wire rack. Makes about 48 cookies.

Chicken Cacciatori

1	3-pound cut-up broiler-fryer chicken
1/2	cup all purpose flour
1/4	cup vegetable oil
1	medium green bell pepper
2	medium onions
2	garlic cloves, minced
1	can (16 ounces) whole tomatoes
1	can (8 ounces) tomato sauce
1	cup sliced mushrooms
1/2	teaspoon dried oregano
1/4	teaspoon dried basil
1/2	teaspoon salt
	Grated Parmesan cheese

Season chicken lightly with salt and pepper. Dredge in flour. Heat oil in large skillet. Cook chicken about 15 minutes each side until browned. Drain. Cut peppers and onions in half. Add all remaining ingredients except the Parmesan cheese. Break up the tomatoes. Heat to a boil, then reduce heat to a simmer and cook covered for 30-45 minutes. Serve with pasta and cheese. Serves 4-6.

Roast Beef
and Yorkshire Pudding

1	beef rib roast (4-5 ribs or 8-9 pounds) preferably from small end of ribs
2	tablespoons olive oil
1	tablespoon Kosher salt
1	teaspoon freshly ground black pepper
1	teaspoon dried oregano
1	teaspoon dried thyme

Preheat oven to 450°. Lightly rub olive oil over entire roast. Liberally sprinkle with the salt pepper and spices. Place roast bone side down in a large roasting pan. Roast at 450° for 15 minutes. Reduce oven temperature to 250°. Roast for an additional 20-30 minutes per pound. Check internal temperature of meat towards the end of cooking time. It should read 130° for rare, 140° for medium rare, 150° for medium. Insert thermometer into thickest part of meat but do not touch the bone. Remove from oven, cover with foil and let rest 20 minutes. Remove all but 3 tablespoons of fat from the roasting pan. Over medium heat on stove top, add 1 can beef broth, scraping up browned bits from bottom of pan. Cook 1-2 minutes. Carve roast into 3/4 inch slices. Strain and serve hot with roast along with a horseradish cream sauce. Serves 6.

Yorkshire Pudding

After removing roast from oven to rest, heat oven to 450°.

1	cup sifted all-purpose flour
1/2	teaspoon salt
2	eggs
1	cup whole milk
1/4	cup roast drippings or oil

Gradually beat the eggs and milk into the flour and salt until you have a smooth batter. Beat well and leave to stand. Pour a little oil or drippings (about 2 teaspoons) into each cup of a heavy gauge muffin tin (I use a cast iron American Popover Pan). Place in the hot oven to preheat for 5 minutes. Beat the batter again and decant into a jug for speed. Without allowing the oil to cool, divide the batter into the hot pans, half filling the cups. Bake for 20-40 minutes - depending on size - until puffed and golden. Serve immediately. Makes 6-8 puddings. Try not to open the oven door until they're done - glass doors are useful. If you have to, just open it enough to take a quick peek.

Gingerbread cottage on Martha's Vineyard

Chatham, Cape Cod

ASPARAGUS WITH HOLLANDAISE SAUCE

1	pound fresh asparagus
2	egg yolks
1	teaspoon fresh lemon juice
2	teaspoons water
2	teaspoons Dijon mustard
1	teaspoon chopped fresh parsley
	Salt and pepper to taste
	Dash of hot pepper sauce
1	stick butter (1/2 cup)

Bring a pot of salted water to a boil. Trim asparagus and place in water. Simmer 4-6 minutes. Remove from water. Keep warm. While asparagus is cooking, prepare the sauce. In a stainless steel bowl set over a pot of simmering water, whisk the egg yolks with the lemon juice, water, mustard and parsley. Season with the salt, pepper and hot sauce. Whisk until mixture is pale yellow and thickened. Do not let the bowl touch the simmering water in pot. When thickened somewhat, remove bowl from pot and while whisking add the butter, small pieces at a time until all is incorporated. Place asparagus on a warm platter and pour over the Hollandaise sauce. Serves 4.

● ● ● ● ● ● ● ● ● ● ● ● ● ● ●

LEMON POUND CAKE

2	sticks butter, softened
1 3/4	cups flour
1/2	teaspoon baking powder
1/2	teaspoon salt
1/4	cup sour cream
1 1/2	tablespoons lemon juice
1 1/2	tablespoons grated lemon peel
1	cup plus 2 tablespoons sugar
5	large eggs, room temperature, beaten

Preheat oven to 325°. Prepare a loaf pan, 9" x 5" by greasing and flouring. Sift together the flour, baking powder, and salt into a bowl. In a second bowl, stir together the sour cream and lemon juice. In the mixing bowl of electric mixer, mix together the lemon peel and sugar. Add the butter and beat for 3-4 minutes. Scrape down sides of bowl occasionally. Add the beaten eggs in 3 additions. Beat well. Lower mixer speed and add the dry ingredients along with the sour cream mixture. Mix just until all is blended, scraping down bowl occasionally. Pour batter in loaf pan and bake 55-65 minutes until a toothpick inserted in center comes out with a few crumbs attached. While cake bakes, make syrup to pour over the top. In a small saucepan, heat 1/4 cup granulated sugar and 1/4 cup lemon juice until sugar dissolves. Cook about 2 minutes. Set aside. Cool cake on rack for 10 minutes. Turn out onto rack and brush sides and top with the syrup. Let cool completely. Serves 8.

SPAGHETTI PIE

1	pound ground round steak
1/4	teaspoon salt
1/4	teaspoon black pepper
2	(8-ounce) cans tomato sauce
1 1/2	cups low-fat sour cream
1/2	cup chopped green onions
1	3-ounce package low-fat cream cheese
8	ounces spaghetti, cooked
1 1/3	cups shredded sharp Cheddar cheese

Preheat oven to 350°. Brown meat in a large skillet. Drain off any fat. Stir in the salt, pepper and tomato sauce. Bring to a boil, reduce heat and simmer 20 minutes. Combine the sour cream, green onions, and cream cheese in a small bowl. Set aside. Place the spaghetti in a 2-quart casserole dish coated with cooking spray. Spread the sour cream mixture over the spaghetti, top with the meat. Sprinkle with the cheddar cheese. Cover and bake for 25 minutes. Uncover and bake an additional 5-10 minutes so cheese can brown. Serves 6.

● ● ● ● ● ● ● ● ● ● ● ● ● ● ●

CRANBERRY FLUFF SALAD

2	cups fresh cranberries, finely chopped
3	cups miniature marshmallows
3/4	cup sugar
2	cups diced apples
1 1/2	cups seedless green grapes, cut in half
1/2	cup coarsely chopped walnuts
1/4	teaspoon salt
1	cup whipping cream, whipped

Combine the cranberries, marshmallows and sugar in a bowl. Cover and chill overnight. Just before serving, stir in the apples, grapes, walnuts, salt. Then fold in the whipped cream. Serves 6.

South Beach, Martha's Vineyard

Roast Duck

1   **4-5 pound duck**
1   **orange, sliced into quarters**
         Salt, pepper & poultry seasoning

Preheat oven to 425°. Wash duck in cold water and remove excess fat. Season the inside cavity and the outside of duck with salt, pepper and poultry seasoning. Place orange quarters inside duck and place in a shallow roasting pan. Bake for 30 minutes, and then remove duck from oven and prick breast with heavy tine kitchen fork to drain grease. Turn oven down to 300° and return duck to oven for 1 hour or 1 hour and 15 minutes.

Orange Sauce:
1/2   cup sugar
1   tablespoon wine vinegar
         Juice of 2 oranges
         1 bay leaf
1/2   teaspoon thyme leaves
         Salt & pepper to taste
1/2   cup Grand Marnier (orange-flavored liquor)
         Grated rind of 1 orange

In a heavy saucepan, combine sugar and wine vinegar. Cook the mixture over a medium flame until sugar melts and begins to caramelize. Add the juice of 2 oranges, Grand Marnier and grated orange rind. Stir well and cook for five minutes. Add 1/4 cup orange peel cut into julienne strips, cooked in a little water for five minutes and drained. Correct the seasonings and pour over the duckling on a serving platter. Serve with yam-stuffed oranges.

with Orange Sauce

EASY ITALIAN SOUP

1 1/2	pounds Italian sausages cut into slices
2	cloves minced garlic.
1	large can (28 ounces) tomatoes
2	cups dry red wine
4	cups beef broth
1/2	teaspoon each dried oregano and basil
1 1/2	cups diced zucchini
2	tablespoons freshly chopped parsley
2	cups cooked bowtie pasta
	Parmesan cheese

In a large Dutch oven, sauté the sausages with the garlic until browned. Add the remaining ingredients except zucchini, parsley and pasta. Simmer for 25 minutes. Add the zucchini and pasta and cook an additional 5 minutes. Serve with garnish of parsley and offer Parmesan cheese as a topping. Serves 6.

● ● ● ● ● ● ● ● ● ● ● ● ● ● ● ● ● ●

LINGUINE WITH MUSSELS AND RED SAUCE

48	medium-sized mussels, scrubbed and debearded
2	tablespoons cornmeal
1	tablespoon olive oil
1/2	cup finely chopped onion
1	garlic clove, minced
1	cup dry white wine
2	tablespoons chopped fresh basil
1/4	teaspoon red pepper flakes
1	28-ounce can plum tomatoes
2	8-ounce cans tomato sauce
1	pound linguine, cooked
1/4	cup chopped fresh parsley

Put mussels in a large bowl of cold water. Sprinkle with the cornmeal and let stand 30-40 minutes. Drain and rinse. Discard the cornmeal. Heat the oil in a large Dutch oven until hot. Add onion and garlic and cook 5 minutes. Add wine and bring to a boil. Cook 5 minutes. Add the basil, pepper, tomatoes and tomato sauce, reduce heat and simmer 10 minutes. Spread mussels over the tomato mixture. Cover and cook over high heat for 3-5 minutes or until mussels open. Discard any mussels that do not open. Divide the linguine into 6 bowls. Divide the mussels and sauce and pour over linguine. Top with the parsley and serve. Serves 8.

HOLIDAY LIVER PATÉ

1	cup butter
1	pound chicken livers
1	medium onion, chopped
1/2	teaspoon curry powder
1/2	teaspoon paprika
1	teaspoon fresh thyme leaves
1/2	teaspoon fresh chopped sage
1/4	teaspoon salt
1/8	teaspoon pepper
2	tablespoons cognac or brandy

Melt 1/4 cup butter in skillet and add all other ingredients but the remaining butter and cognac. Cook over low heat for 8-10 minutes. Pour the mixture in a blender. Add the remaining butter and cognac and blend until smooth. (Be careful when blending hot liquids in a blender as it expands and will blow off the lid if not done in slow pulses at the beginning). Put into crocks and store in the refrigerator. Keeps in refrigerator 4-5 days. This also freezes well. Makes 2 cups paté.

● ● ● ● ● ● ● ● ● ● ● ● ● ● ● ● ● ●

CROCK POT APPLE BUTTER

	Apples, peeled, cored and finely chopped
3-4	cups sugar
4	teaspoons cinnamon
1/4	teaspoon ground cloves
1/4	teaspoon salt

Fill crock pot heaping full. Drizzle with sugar and spices. Cover and cook on high for 1 hour, lower heat and cook all day until thick. Stir occasionally. Seal in jars. This freezes well.

Nobska Lighthouse, Cape Cod

Boiled Lobster

It is important to select a pot big enough to hold enough water to cover the lobsters completely. Bring the water to a rolling boil and add 1 tablespoon salt per quart of water. Put the lobsters in claws first and begin timing from the moment the water comes back to a boil.

To steam lobsters, cook them, covered, in a steamer basket above boiling water. They will need 1 to 2 minutes less, as the steam is hotter than boiling water.

For 1 pound: 5 minutes
1 1/8 pounds: 6 minutes
1 1/4 pounds: 8 minutes
1 1/2 to 2 pounds: 8 to 10 minutes
More than 2 pounds : 12 minutes

Historians believe that Vikings visited the fertile fishing waters off the coast of present-day Maine as early as A.D. 1000 and that European fisherman discovered the area long before English settlers arrived to establish the short-lived Popham Plantation in 1607. During the 1620s, several permanent settlements were established and for more that a hundred years, cod fishing was the principal industry. In the next century, smoked mackerel and herring became the most prominent fish product. In the 1870s, the development of the canning industry expanded the market for Maine fish to homes across the country. About the same time, commercial lobster fishing was thriving. The popularity of lobster nearly led to its demise as lobster beds depleted dramatically. Strict conservation methods have restored the lobster industry.

Although agriculture plays only a small role in Maine's economy, there are a few valuable crops including potatoes, blueberries, apples and maple syrup. Most of the income of Maine farmers comes from livestock and livestock products, especially milk and eggs. Forest products, limestone, granite, sand and gravel also contribute to the economy. Culinary curiosities include bean-hole-beans, a legacy from the Penobscot Indians, in which beans are cooked in a cast-iron pot underground in a hole.

Millions of tourists visit Maine each year to vacation along the rocky shores and rugged beauty of the Atlantic coastline. Inland, hunters stalk bears, deer and other game animals while sports fishermen can try their luck in 2,500 lakes and ponds and 5,000 rivers and streams. Skiers, hikers and climbers enjoy Maine's mountains. Historic sites and many annual festivals are also popular among visitors.

Portland Head Lighthouse, Cape Elizabeth, MN

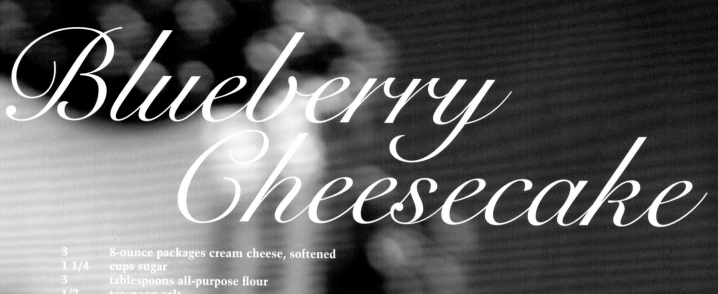

Blueberry Cheesecake

3	8-ounce packages cream cheese, softened
1 1/4	cups sugar
3	tablespoons all-purpose flour
1/2	teaspoon salt
4	large eggs
1	cup sour cream
1	teaspoon vanilla
1	tablespoon grated lemon rind

Crust

1 1/2	cups finely ground almonds
1/4	cup sugar
3	tablespoons butter, softened
1	tablespoon flour

Mix all ingredients in a small bowl. Press into a 9-inch springform pan, extending 1 inch up the sides.

Topping

1/3	cup all-fruit blueberry spread
12	ounces fresh blueberries or 12-ounce package frozen blueberries, thawed, drained.

Beat cream cheese at medium speed until smooth. Add the sugar, flour and salt and blend well. Add the eggs, one at a time, beating well after each addition. Add the sour cream, vanilla and lemon rind, beating just until blended. Pour batter into pan. Bake in a preheated 350° oven for 1 hour and 10 minutes or until center is firm. Turn off oven and open oven door. Leave cake in oven for 30 minutes with door open. Remove and cool completely. Refrigerate for several hours to chill completely before serving. Top with the blueberry topping and serve. Serves 12-14.

PUMPKIN CHEESE BARS

Crust:

1	cup all-purpose flour
1/2	cup packed brown sugar
1/4	teaspoon salt
1	stick butter, cold and cut into small pieces
1	cup chopped walnuts
3/4	cup old-fashioned oats

Filling:

1	8-ounce package cream cheese, softened
3/4	cup canned pumpkin, not pie mix
1/2	cup sugar
1	egg
1	teaspoon ground cinnamon
1/2	teaspoon ground ginger
1/4	teaspoon ground allspice

Topping:

1	cup sour cream
3	tablespoons sugar
1/2	teaspoon vanilla extract

Crust: Preheat oven to 350°. Butter a 9-inch square pan. Combine the flour, brown sugar, salt in a bowl. Add the butter and cut into the dry ingredients until mixture resembles coarse meal. Add the nuts and oats. Press 3/4 of mixture into prepared pan. Spread remaining crumbs on a cookie sheet. Bake until golden. Do not let crumbs burn. Remove from oven to cool. Bake crust in preheated oven for 25 – 30 minutes. Let cool 10 minutes. Leave oven on.

Filling: Blend all ingredients and spread the filling over the crust and bake about 20 minutes or until filling is set.

Topping: Mix ingredients for topping. Spread over hot filling. Bake an additional 5 minutes. Gently press in the remaining crumbs from crust and chill bars thoroughly.

• • • • • • • • • • • • • •

ITALIANS
(Known as hoagies, heroes, grinders and submarines in other parts of the country)

"Italians" are typically made without mustard, mayonnaise or lettuce. They are made with a freshly baked soft roll, not a crusty one and include vegetables such as chopped onions, bell peppers and olives (green and/or black), a variety of cold cuts such as ham, salami and cheese. Instead of mayonnaise, the layers of meat and vegetables are topped with salt and pepper, a squirt of olive oil and a sour pickle.

GINGER SNAP COOKIES

3/4	cup butter
1	cup sugar
1/2	cup molasses
1	egg
2	cups flour
1	teaspoon baking soda
1/2	teaspoon salt
1	teaspoon cinnamon
1	teaspoon ground cloves
1	teaspoon ground ginger

Preheat oven to 375°. In mixing bowl, combine the butter, sugar, molasses and egg. Sift together the dry ingredients and slowly add to butter and sugar mixture. Form into 1 1/2- inch balls and roll in granulated sugar. Place 2 inches apart on a cookie sheet. Bake 8 minutes for a chewy cookie and 10 minutes for a crisp cookie. Makes 36.

• • • • • • • • • • • • • •

MAINE MAPLE TAFFY

What is maple taffy? It's a concentrate of pure maple syrup poured over packed snow until it hardens, then is picked up with a spoon or eaten like a lollypop.

8	ounces of pure maple syrup
1	ball of snow the size of a small snowball (for test)

Fill a large saucepan filled with packed, clean snow. Pour the maple syrup into a deep pot and bring to a boil. If it threatens to bubble over, place one or two drops of vegetable oil in the boiling syrup. Boil for 4 minutes, and then test the syrup by pouring a small amount onto the small snowball. If it clings to the snow and stops running, it's ready. Slowly pour the syrup in short, thin lines onto the packed snow that you've prepared ahead in a separate saucepan.

Maine in the fall of the year

Apple Coffee Cake

2	medium tart apples (Granny Smith)
2	cups all-purpose flour
2 1/4	teaspoons baking powder
2	teaspoons ground cinnamon
1/2	teaspoon salt
1/2	cup butter
1	cup sugar
1/2	cup milk
2	large eggs
1	teaspoon vanilla
1/3	cup apple or currant jelly, heated

Preheat oven to 450°. Grease and flour an 8-inch by 3-inch springform pan. Peel and core the apples. Cut into 1/2-inch slices.

Mix the dry ingredients in a small bowl. Set aside. In the mixer bowl, beat the butter until smooth. Add the sugar and beat until fluffy. Beat in the milk, eggs and vanilla. Slowly add the dry ingredients and beat on medium speed until smooth. Spread the batter in the prepared pan. Arrange the apple slices on top in a circular pattern. Brush with 1/2 the jelly that has been heated. Reduce the oven temperature to 350°. Bake for 50-60 minutes or until a toothpick inserted in center comes out clean. Do not allow cake to overbake. Start to test after cake has baked 45 minutes. Cool cake for 20 minutes then remove from pan. Brush with remaining jelly. Cool completely.

Lobster Rolls

This popular Maine sandwich couldn't be easier!

3 ounces of cooked lobster meat for each roll
   Mayonnaise
   Choice of dinner rolls

Cut the cooked lobster meat into bite size pieces. Mix with mayonnaise to desired consistency. Place in dinner roll. Traditional Maine lobster rolls are often made with fresh hot dog rolls, but any dinner roll will do. Eat as is, or butter both sides of the roll and grill in a frying pan until golden brown.

• • • • • • • • • • • • •

Blueberry Muffins

1 1/2	cups flour
1/4	cup sugar
2	teaspoons baking powder
1/4	teaspoon salt
1	large egg
1/2	cup milk
1 1/2	cups blueberries
1	tablespoon butter
1/2	teaspoon grated lemon peel

Preheat oven to 375°. Lightly spray muffin tins with oil. Mix flour, sugar, baking powder and salt in a large bowl and set aside. Whisk egg with the milk and butter. Add the dry ingredients and mix until just blended. Gently stir in the blueberries. Fill the muffin tins 2/3 cup full and bake in preheated oven 15-20 minutes. Cool 5 minutes before removing from pan.

• • • • • • • • • • • • •

Blueberry Slump

(Also known as Blueberry Grunt)

2	cups fresh Maine wild blueberries
1/2	cup sugar
1	cup water
1	cup sifted flour
2	teaspoons baking powder
1/4	teaspoon salt
1/2	cup milk

Combine blueberries, sugar, and water in a saucepan and stew them over medium heat. Mix flour, baking powder and salt in a bowl. Add milk to the dry mixture stirring quickly to make dumpling dough that will drop from the end of a spoon. When sauce is boiling, drop dumplings (about 1 to 2 inches in size) into it. Lower heat a little and cover pan tightly. Cook for about 20 minutes. Spoon dumplings into shallow bowls and cover them with sauce. Top with cream or whipped cream if desired. Serves 4.

Lobster Thermador

4	whole live Maine lobsters, about 1-1/2 pounds each
1/3	cup unsalted butter
3	tablespoons flour
1	teaspoon salt
1/8	teaspoon freshly ground nutmeg
1/8	teaspoon paprika
1	cup half-and-half
3	tablespoons dry white wine
1/2	cup finely grated cheddar cheese
1	quartered lemon
4	sprigs parsley

Heat 3-4 gallons water to boil in a stockpot, over a high flame. Plunge lobsters into boiling water. When water comes to a boil, cover and simmer for 12-13 minutes. Remove from pot and drain well. Remove claws and legs, leaving body intact. Remove flesh from claws and legs, and set aside. Cut thin undershell from tail with shears and gently remove flesh from tail shell. Cut flesh to large dice and combine with flesh from claws. Wash shells well and drain. Heat butter in a saucepan. Whisk in flour, salt and nutmeg. Heat and stir until bubbly. Whisk in half-and-half and wine. Add lobster and stir to coat well. Remove from heat. Invert shells onto a broiler pan and fill with lobster mixture. Top with grated cheddar cheese. Place in broiler briefly to melt cheese and brown lightly. Remove to a serving platter. Garnish with wedges and parsley. Serve hot!

• • • • • • • • • • • • •

Scalloped Oysters

1	pint oysters
2	cup cracker crumbs
1/2	cup butter, melted
3/4	cup light cream
1/4	cup oyster liquid
1/4	teaspoon Worcestershire sauce
1/2	teaspoon salt

Preheat oven to 350°. Drain oysters, reserve 1/4 cup liquid. Combine cracker crumbs and butter. Spread 1/2 of crumbs in greased pan. Cover with 1/2 of oysters. Sprinkle with pepper. Spread another 1/2 of crumbs and remaining oysters. Sprinkle with pepper. Combine cream and liquid with Worcestershire sauce and salt. Pour over oysters. Top with rest of crumbs. Bake for 40 minutes. Serves 4.

Grilled Lobster Tail

1/2	cup butter, melted
2	tablespoons fresh lemon juice
1/2	cup olive oil
2	teaspoons paprika
1	teaspoon salt
1/4	teaspoon pepper
4	lobster tails (8 to 10 oz. each)

Preheat a gas grill for high heat or prepare a charcoal grill with hot coals. Lightly oil the grate or spray it with non-stick cooking spray. Using a strong kitchen shears or a large butcher knife, split the lobster tails lengthwise. Whisk the melted butter and olive oil together in a small bowl. Whisk in the lemon juice, paprika, salt and pepper. Brush the meat on the 8 lobster tail halves with the marinade. Let stand for about 3 to 5 minutes, then place the lobster tail halves, meaty side down, on the preheated grill. Grill for about 10 to 12 minutes, turning after about 5 or 6 minutes, and baste the lobster meat with the remaining marinade. The lobster tails are done when the meat is opaque. Serves 4.

BLUEBERRY CORNMEAL PANCAKES

1-1/2	cups coarse yellow cornmeal
1/4	cup whole wheat flour
1/4	cup oat bran
1	teaspoon baking soda
1/2	teaspoon salt
2	tablespoons pure maple syrup
2	tablespoons vegetable oil
2	cups low-fat buttermilk
1	egg, lightly beaten
1-1/2	cups small fresh or frozen blueberries

Combine cornmeal, flour, oat bran, soda, and salt in medium bowl. In a small bowl, combine syrup, oil, egg, and buttermilk. Stir well and add to dry ingredients. Let batter stand for 15 minutes to soften cornmeal. Add additional milk if required for proper consistency. Pour batter onto griddle and sprinkle with blueberries. Turn when tops are bubbly. Yields 12 5-inch pancakes.

● ● ● ● ● ● ● ● ● ● ● ● ● ● ● ●

TARRAGON-PECAN SALMON

4	6-ounce salmon fillets
2	teaspoons finely grated orange zest
1/4	cup orange juice
2	tablespoons olive oil
2	teaspoons chopped fresh tarragon
1	tablespoon Dijon mustard
1	tablespoon butter
1	teaspoon honey
1/4	cup dry breadcrumbs
1/4	cup finely chopped pecans
1	tablespoon finely chopped fresh parsley
2	teaspoons finely chopped fresh tarragon

Preheat oven to 425°. Rinse fillets. Pat dry with paper towels. Place fish in a plastic bag in a deep bowl. Combine the orange zest, juice, olive oil and 2 teaspoons fresh tarragon. Pour over fish and let stand at room temperature for 20 minutes. In a small bowl, combine the mustard, butter and honey. Set aside. In another dish, combine the breadcrumbs, pecans, parsley and remaining 2 teaspoons fresh tarragon. Remove salmon from marinade and discard the marinade. Place fish skin side down on a greased shallow baking pan. Brush with the mustard mixture. Sprinkle with the crumb mixture, pressing into salmon. Bake, uncovered, for 12-16 minutes or until fish flakes. When serving, sprinkle each serving with more fresh parsley. Serves 4.

CHICKEN KIEV

1	cup butter
2	tablespoons snipped parsley
1 1/2	teaspoons dried tarragon leaves
1	teaspoon. chives
1	teaspoon. salt
1/8	teaspoon pepper
4	whole chicken breasts, boned, split and skin removed
1	cup flour
4	eggs, well beaten
2	cups dry bread crumbs

Blend butter, parsley, tarragon, chives, salt and pepper. Shape into 4-inch square on aluminum foil. Wrap and freeze until firm, 30-40 minutes. Place chicken breasts between 2 pieces waxed paper; pound to 1/4-inch thickness, being careful not to make holes in meat. Cut frozen butter square into 8 pieces. Place 1 piece butter in the center of each chicken breast. Fold chicken over butter, making sure butter is completely sealed inside chicken. Fasten with wooden toothpicks. Roll chicken in flour, dip in eggs, and coat with bread crumbs; repeat. Refrigerate for 1-2 hours. Heat vegetable oil in deep fat fryer 3-4 inch deep to 360 degrees. Fry chicken pieces 2 pieces at a time, until a deep golden brown, about 8 minutes, turning, if necessary; drain. Keep warm in a 275° oven until all are cooked and ready to serve. Serves 6.

Maine in the Spring

Sautéed Scallops with Garlic

2	tablespoons extra virgin olive oil
3	tablespoons butter
2	pounds sea scallops, cut in half horizontally if very large
	Flour for dredging
	Salt and pepper to taste
1	tablespoon minced garlic
	Chopped fresh parsley leaves, or chives, for garnish

Put the oil and butter in a large nonstick skillet and turn the heat to medium-high. Dry the scallops. Dredge the scallops lightly in the flour. When the butter foam subsides, add the scallops swiftly but not all at once. Turn them individually, as they brown, allowing about 2 minutes per side. Season with salt and pepper as they cook. Once you have turned all the scallops, add the garlic and lower the heat a bit. Stir or, even better, shake the pan gently so the garlic cooks a bit and is distributed among the scallops. Garnish and serve. These are a perfect addition to pasta.

LOBSTER STEW

4	tablespoons butter
1/2	medium onion, finely chopped
2	cups cooked lobster meat, cut into bite-size pieces
2	cups cream
2	cups half-and-half
2	tablespoons sherry
	Salt and pepper to taste
	Parsley for garnish

Sauté the onion in the butter until translucent. Add the lobster and sauté for another minute or so. Add the cream, half-and-half and heat through. Just before serving add the sherry. Ladle into serving bowls and garnish with chopped parsley. Serves 4-6.

● ● ● ● ● ● ● ● ● ● ● ● ● ● ●

FINNAN HADDIE

A traditional dish with origins in Scotland

1	large shallot
1/4	cup butter
3	tablespoons flour
1	pound Finnan Haddie
1/2	cup Scotch whiskey
1	cup heavy cream
2	cups fish stock (fish bouillon)
4	large potatoes, peeled and boiled

Put the smoked fish in a pan and cover with water. Bring to a boil over medium heat and cook for 10 minutes. Remove from the pan and drain. Remove the skin and bones and flake the fish. Sauté the fillet and chopped shallot in the butter until the shallots are transparent. Add flour and cook for two minutes over medium heat. Add Scotch and cook an additional minute to release alcohol. Add heated fish stock and whisk until smooth. Bring to a boil and add heated cream. Boil again, lower heat, and cook slowly to desired consistency. Serve over warmed, cooked potatoes. Serves 4.

FIDDLEHEADS

Fiddleheads are a Maine spring delicacy. They appear on menus and in markets in the region from about May through early July. What exactly are these deep green, coiled vegetables? Fiddleheads are actually young fern fronds that have not yet opened up. They must be picked during a two-week window before the fern unfurls. Fiddleheads are named for their appearance, which resembles the scroll at the head or top of a fiddle. Fiddleheads can be consumed raw or cooked.

Clean, Clean, Clean! Fiddleheads. To clean fresh fiddleheads, rinse several times in fresh water, swirling the fiddleheads with your hands to work out the brown leaf like covering that protects the fiddlehead from early spring frosts!

● ● ● ● ● ● ● ● ● ● ● ● ● ● ●

CREAMY FIDDLEHEAD SOUP

1 1/2	cups fiddleheads, chopped
2	chicken bouillon cubes
1/2	cup finely chopped onion
2	tablespoons butter
4	cups half and half cream
	Salt and pepper to taste

Melt butter and bouillon cubes in a saucepan and sauté the onions and fiddleheads for 10 minutes. Add the half and half and heat through. Season to taste with salt and pepper. Serve hot. Serves 6-8.

Boothbay Harbor, Maine

Old Fashioned Potato Salad

1	cup mayonnaise
1	teaspoon dry mustard
1/4	teaspoon pepper
4	medium potatoes, cooked and diced
4	hard-boiled eggs, chopped
1	cup celery, chopped
1/4	cup onion, chopped

Mix mayonnaise, mustard and pepper in a large bowl. Add remaining ingredients; mix lightly. Refrigerate. Makes 8 servings.

Booth Bay Harbor, Maine

Nubble Light, Maine

The mountains, lakes and streams of Vermont were rich hunting grounds for Indians before white explorers and settlers arrived. In the early 1600s, Samuel de Champlain claimed the region for France. Following the French and Indian War (1754 – 1763), England gained control for a few years until 1777 when Vermont declared itself an independent republic. After the American colonists defeated the British and formed the United States in 1783, Vermont retained its independence until 1791 when it joined the Union as the 14th state.

Farming became an important but minor contributor to Vermont's economy. Dairy farming and dairy products are the chief agricultural activity. Cheese makers produce an impressive variety of specialty cheeses that rank among the nation's finest. Likewise, Vermont is famous for producing maple syrup and maple sugar. Potatoes are the leading vegetable while apples are the leading fruit.

Manufacturing is the most important economic activity in Vermont, as it is in other New England states, and tourism is the largest industry. Vermont's mountains and forests attract many skiers, hikers, hunters and other outdoor enthusiasts. Visitors pour into the autumn countryside to see brilliant yellow, orange, purple and red colors of turning leaves. Real estate is a primary service industry because many families from New York and Massachusetts purchase vacation homes in Vermont.

Maple Walnut Ice Cream
with Chocolate Sauce

4	egg yolks
3	cups heavy cream
3/4	cup chopped walnuts
1	cup Grade B Maple Syrup

Beat egg yolks. In a heavy saucepan, bring the cream to a boil. Slowly whisk the heated cream into the eggs. Cool completely. Mix in the maple syrup just before freezing in an ice cream machine. When almost done, stir in walnut pieces. Makes 1 quart.

Dark Chocolate Sauce:

1/3	cup water
1/2	cup unsweetened cocoa powder
1/2	cup firmly packed dark brown sugar
2	tablespoon butter
1/2	teaspoon vanilla

Heat water and sugar in a heavy saucepan. Whisk constantly until sugar is dissolved. Add the cocoa powder and whisk until smooth. Add the butter and vanilla. Remove from heat and cool. Makes 1 cup sauce.

APPLE CHEDDAR SMOKED BRATWURST CANAPÉS

3	medium-sized Granny Smith apples
1	pound Vermont Cabot Cheddar cheese
1/3	cup honey
1/4	cup Dijon mustard
2	slices rye cocktail bread, crumbled (stale or toasted)
2	tablespoons caraway seed
1-1/4	cups mayonnaise
1-1/2	loaves rye cocktail bread, sliced, slices cut in half to make triangles
3/4	pound smoked bratwurst, sliced thin.

After peeling and grating the apple, squeeze out the excess juice. Drink the fresh juice and blend the cheese with the remaining ingredients. Mix ingredients together. Slice bratwurst and lay onto bread triangles and mound apple cheddar mixture and quickly roast in a preheated 375-400 degree-oven until golden brown, about 7-8 minutes. Serve and enjoy.

- -

APPLE SPICE CAKE

3	cups flour
1/2	teaspoon salt
1	teaspoon baking soda
1	teaspoon cinnamon
1	teaspoon allspice
3	eggs
2	cups sugar
1	cup oil
2	teaspoons vanilla
3	cups finely chopped apples
1	cup chopped nuts

Sift together flour, salt, soda and spices. Mix in a separate bowl the eggs, sugar, oil and vanilla. Add to dry ingredients. Add chopped apples and nuts. Pour into greased and floured bundt pan. Bake at 350 degrees for 1 hour and 15 minutes or until toothpick inserted in center of thickest part of cake comes out clean.

Frosting:

1/2	cup (1 stick) unsalted butter, room temp.
4	ounce cream cheese, room temp.
1	cup sifted powdered sugar
1/2	cup pure maple syrup
3/4	cup chopped pecans

For frosting: Cream butter and cream cheese until smooth. Add sugar and maple syrup and mix until smooth. Stir chopped pecans into frosting. Spread frosting on cake. (Can be prepared 1 day ahead. Cover and refrigerate.) Serve at room temperature. 12 servings.

CHOCOLATE CREME BRULEE

2	cups heavy cream
1/3	cup chocolate liqueur
4	egg yolks
3/4	cup sugar
1/4	cup sugar (for topping)

Preheat oven to 325°. Bring the heavy cream and liquor to a boil and remove from heat. Whisk together the egg yolks and first sugar (3/4 cup). Temper the egg mixture into the cream mixture. Pour into 4-ounce ramekins to the top. Place ramekins into a larger cake pan and pour hot water 1/2 of the way up the ramekin. Bake in a 325° oven for 45 minutes to an hour (firm to the touch). Remove them from the pan and cool to room temperature. Sprinkle a generous amount of sugar on the top and brown off under your broiler or use a torch. Let the melted and browned sugar set for a few minutes before serving. Serves 4.

- -

CORN FRITTERS WITH VERMONT MAPLE SYRUP

2	cups fresh corn, scraped from the cob
2	eggs
1/2	teaspoon salt
2	tablespoons flour (or less)
1	teaspoon sugar
1	tablespoon butter, melted
	Vegetable oil

Mix all ingredients except oil together. Heat oil in cast iron skillet to cover 1/4 inch and add large spoonfuls of batter. Cook 3 to 4 minutes per side. Flatten with a spatula after turning. Amount of flour can vary. If the corn is very milky and wet, use more flour; batter should not be runny. Serve with real Vermont maple syrup. This dish can be served as a vegetable or a main vegetarian course. Serves 4.

Pork with Apples & Cream

4	medium apples (they should be of a drier variety such as Jonagold, Cortland)
1	tablespoon sugar
2	tenderloins of pork sliced thickly on the diagonal into 6 pieces
1	large chopped onion
	Unsalted butter
5	tablespoons or 1/3 cup Vermont Apple Brandy
1	tablespoon flour
2/3	bottle of Vermont Hard Cider
1	cup chicken stock
2/3	cup crème fraiche
	Lemon
	Salt and pepper to taste

Peel and slice apples thickly. Sauté in butter over low medium heat to lightly brown and slightly soften. Sprinkle sugar over the slices raising the heat to caramelize. Set pan aside.Season the pork with salt and pepper. Using two sauté pans, melt a generous lump of butter in each and divide the chopped onion, cooking until translucent. Add the meat and brown on all sides. Pour on all but 1 large tablespoon of brandy. Warm the ladle of brandy and then light it, pouring over the meat in both pans to flame, stir until the flame dies down.

Sprinkle the flour over each pan, sautéing a few more minutes and de-glaze with the hard cider and stock, stirring to dissolve any lumps. Cover and simmer, turning the pieces of meat over occasionally. Meat juices will run clear when the meat is fully cooked; pork will be just pink.

Remove pork to a warmed serving dish. Gently re-heat the sautéed apple. Combine the sauce and further reduce in one pan, lower heat and add the cream, season with salt and freshly ground pepper to taste and a squeeze of lemon. Arrange the apples around the pork, and then pour the sauce over all. Serves 6-8.

A few thousand peaceful Algonquain Indian families hunted, fished and farmed in what is now Rhode Island. The first permanent white settlement was founded in 1636 at Providence. More colonists moved into the area and established farms in the fertile coastal region. However, with limited amount of land for agriculture, Rhode Islanders turned to the sea for food and trade. Historic Newport on Narragansett Bay was a major shipping center in the 1700s and became famous in the late 1800s as a summer resort and seasonal home to the ultra wealthy.

Rhode Island's annual fish catch is an important contributor to the state's economic income. The most valuable catch is flounder. The prime shellfish harvest includes quahog and cherrystone clams as well as oysters, scallops and lobsters. As in other New England states, apples are the major fruit and potatoes are the leading crop. Dairy products are a primary source of agricultural income. The state's farmers also raise chickens, eggs and turkeys. The Rhode Island Red, a famous breed of chicken, was developed in the town of Little Compton.

Tourism is a major industry. Although Rhode Island is America's smallest state, it is one of the nation's wealthiest repositories of historical attractions, boasting over 20% of the country's National Historic Landmarks. Thousands of vacationers annually visit the coastal resorts along the beautiful Narragansett Bay and 400 miles of shoreline with white sandy beaches and recreational opportunities including boating, swimming, fishing and other water sports.

Castle Hill Lighthouse, Newport, Rhode Island.

Baked Scrod

1	pound scrod
1/2	cup butter
1/2	cup chopped onion
1/3	cup finely chopped celery
1	teaspoon parsley
1/2	teaspoon dry Italian seasoning
1	teaspoon lemon juice
20	Ritz crackers, crushed

Preheat oven to 350°. Arrange fish in a buttered baking dish. In a skillet, heat the butter over low heat. Add the remaining ingredients except cracker crumbs. Sauté for 15-20 minutes until vegetables are cooked. Pour mixture over the cracker crumbs and mix well. Spoon mixture over the fish. Bake until fish is tender and cooked through and crumbs are lightly browned (about 25-30 minutes). Serves 3-4.

Sally Lunn

3 1/4	cups flour
1	tablespoon active dry yeast
1/2	cup melted shortening
3/4	cup sugar
3/4	cup (plus) milk
1/2	teaspoon of salt
1	egg
4	tablespoons warm water

Grease a cookie sheet. Heat the milk and shortening to lukewarm (110°). Mix flour, salt and sugar in a separate bowl. Add water to the yeast in a separate bowl. Mix the egg in yet another bowl. Add the warm milk and melted shortening to the bowl of flour, salt and sugar. Add the egg and yeast and water. Beat the entire mixture until it comes off the side of the bowl, which should be clean. Cover, let rise in a warm (non-air conditioned) place until double in size, about 1 1/2 hours. Knead the bread down in size and shape into a round loaf. Place on the cookie sheet and let rise again, about 45 minutes. Bake bread in a preheated 325° oven for approximately 45 minutes. After 30 minutes, baste the top of the bread with butter, and also again after it has finished baking.

● ● ● ● ● ● ● ● ● ● ● ● ● ● ●

Indian Pudding

4	cups milk
1/4	cup sugar
1/2	cup molasses
1/2	cup cornmeal
1/4	teaspoon ground allspice
1/4	teaspoon ground nutmeg
1/2	teaspoon ground ginger
1	teaspoon ground cinnamon
1/2	teaspoon salt
2	tablespoons unsalted butter plus extra for buttering the dish
	Vanilla ice cream for topping

Place 3-1/2 cups of the milk in a medium-size saucepan and heat on medium temperature. Stir in the molasses and sugar and when they are thoroughly mixed, turn the heat to low. Preheat oven to 300 degrees.

Slowly sprinkle the cornmeal over the warm milk mixture, whisking until no lumps remain. When the mixture thickens in about 10 minutes, add all remaining ingredients, except the reserved 1/2 cup milk. Turn off the heat. Grease an 8 or 9-inch-baking dish and turn the warm mixture into it; pour remaining milk over the top. Do not stir. Bake 2-1/2 or 3 hours until pudding is set. Serve hot in bowls with a scoop of vanilla ice cream on top. Pudding may also be served chilled and sliced. Makes 8 servings.

Easy Apple Pancakes

1	cup sifted flour
1	teaspoon baking powder
1/2	teaspoon salt
1	egg
3/4	cup milk
1	tablespoon melted butter
1/2	cup finely chopped apple

Sift the dry ingredients together. Combine the egg and milk and add to dry mix. Beat until smooth. Add butter and chopped apple. Bake on a lightly greased hot griddle, turning once. Makes 6 pancakes.

● ● ● ● ● ● ● ● ● ● ● ● ● ● ● ● ● ● ●

Jonny Cakes

1	cup cornmeal
1	teaspoon salt
1	teaspoon sugar
1 1/2	cups boiling water

Combine the dry ingredients in a medium-sized bowl. Add the boiling water, stirring constantly. Mixture will be thick. Heat 1 teaspoon oil in a heavy cast iron skillet until very hot. Drop batter in large spoonfuls onto hot skillet. Cakes should be about 3/4-inch thick and about 3 inches wide. Even out with back of spoon so thickness is uniform. Do not let cakes touch. Fry for 5-6 minutes on each side. Makes 8-10 cakes. Serve hot with butter and maple syrup and/or jam.

● ● ● ● ● ● ● ● ● ● ● ● ● ● ● ● ● ●

Apple Chutney

2	large tart cooking apples (such as green Granny Smith), peeled, cored, and chopped
1/2	cup chopped onion
1/4	cup red wine vinegar
1/4	cup brown sugar
1	tablespoon grated orange peel
1	tablespoon grated fresh ginger
1/2	teaspoon allspice

Combine all ingredients in a medium saucepan and stir well. Bring to a boil; reduce heat and simmer, covered, for 50 minutes. Uncover and simmer over low heat for a few minutes more to cook off excess liquid; let cool. Cover and refrigerate for up to 2 weeks. Makes about 2 cups.

Clam Chowder

In a large pot, bring 1 1/2 cups water to a boil. Add the clams, cover and cook for 3-4 minutes. Stir the clams. Cook an additional 5-7 minutes or until clams have opened. Transfer clams to large bowl and then strain the remaining broth (you should have about 3 cups broth). If not, add water or clam juice (bottled) to make 3 cups. When clams are cool, remove from shells and chop if clams are large. Set broth and clams aside.

In a heavy pot, sauté the bacon until crispy. Add the butter, onions and celery. Cook about 3 minutes. Add the garlic and thyme and cook an additional 2 minutes. Do not let vegetables brown. Add the potatoes and reserved broth. Cover, over low heat cook about 15 minutes or until potatoes are tender. Remove from heat and stir in the clams and cream. Season with salt and pepper. Let rest for 1 hour or so. Slowly reheat but do not boil. Serve with garnish of parsley and onions. Serves 4-6.

5	pounds large cherrystone clams, scrubbed, rinsed and open clams discarded
3	slices bacon, sliced into 1/2" pieces
2	tablespoons butter
1/2	cup chopped onions
1/2	cup chopped celery
1	teaspoon minced garlic
2	springs fresh thyme
2	cups potatoes, peeled and cubed
1	cup heavy cream
1/2	teaspoon salt
1/4	teaspoon black pepper
3	tablespoons chopped fresh parsley
2	tablespoons chopped green onions

Members of the Algonquian Indian tribe hunted and fished in the rugged mountains and sandy shores of present-day New Hampshire for many years prior to the arrival of a Scotsman, two English fish-merchants and a small group of colonists in 1623. The immigrants set up a fishing colony at the mouth of the Piscataqua River. Later arrivals carved farms out of the wilderness and worked the land for food. Early New Hampshire remained rural until the outbreak of the Civil War when an industrial growth began that continues to the present day. Portsmouth, the only town open to the sea, became a major shipbuilding center. By the 1900s, the increasingly urban state suffered depression in their textile and shoe manufacturing industries and by mid-century was mostly replaced by the prosperous electronics industry.

Potatoes, corn and other vegetables are grown in the Merrimack Valley. Fine-flavored apples grow in the hillsides and peaches and berries grow in the southern part of the state. Dairy products account for nearly one-third of the state's total farm income.

Although the coastline is only about 18 miles long, a group of offshore islands, the Isles of Shoals, belong to the state and provide favorable growing conditions for lobsters and other shell fish as well as a wide variety of salt-water fish. In addition to commercial fishing, fish and game are a major factor in the recreation business. New Hampshire offers year-round outdoor activities and attracts millions of visitors annually.

Crab Cakes

1	pound lump crab meat
1	slice bread, crumbled
1	egg
2	tablespoons mayonnaise
1	tablespoon Dijon mustard
1	tablespoon milk
1/2	teaspoon baking powder
1	tablespoon chopped fresh parsley
1	teaspoon Old Bay seasoning
1	teaspoon Worcestershire sauce
	Salt and pepper to taste
	Butter for frying

Gently mix the bread crumbs into the crab meat. In a separate bowl, mix together the egg, mayonnaise, mustard, milk, baking powder, parsley, Old Bay seasoning, Worcestershire sauce and salt and pepper to taste. Add to crab mixture. Heat butter in a large skillet. Form crab into patties and brown on both sides in the butter. Serve with cocktail or tartar sauce. Serves 4-6.

Salmon Pie

1	unbaked pie crust
1	pound potatoes, peeled and sliced
2	large carrots, peeled and sliced
1	large onion, sliced
1	tablespoon butter
2	tablespoons butter
3	tablespoons flour
1/8	teaspoon paprika
3/4	teaspoon salt
1/4	teaspoon pepper
1	cup milk
1/2	pound cooked or canned salmon
1	tablespoon butter
1	egg yolk
1	tablespoon water

Cook the potatoes and carrots in enough water to cover, in a large saucepan for 10 minutes and drain. Do not overcook. Sauté the onion in 1 tablespoon butter until translucent. Melt 2 tablespoons butter in a small saucepan and stir in the flour, paprika, salt and pepper. Blend in the milk and simmer until thickened, stirring constantly. Layer the potato/carrot mixture, salmon and white sauce in a greased 1-quart baking dish (chose a dish that will not be bigger than the pastry). Dot the top with the 1 tablespoon butter. Top with the pastry, sealing the edges. Cut a slit in top center of crust to allow steam to escape. Whisk the egg yolk and water in a small bowl. Brush the top pastry with the egg yolk mixture and bake in a preheated 350° oven for 35-45 minutes or until crust is browned. Serves 4-6.

• • • • • • • • • • • • • • • • • •

Swiss Fondue

Fondue:

2/3	cup white wine or non-alcoholic wine
3	cups (12 ounces) Fanny Mason Baby Swiss or other Baby Swiss or Swiss cheese, shredded
1	tablespoon cornstarch
	Accompaniments: Bread cubes, sliced vegetables (asparagus, broccoli, carrots, zucchini, baby new potatoes)

Bring wine to a boil in a fondue pot over high heat. Combine cheese and cornstarch in mixing bowl. Reduce heat to low; gradually add cheese mixture, whisking constantly until melted and smooth. Keep fondue warm over a low flame.

Old Portsmouth Orange Cake

1	cup sugar
5	eggs
2	tablespoons orange juice
2	tablespoons water
1	tablespoon grated orange rind
1/4	teaspoon orange extract
1/2	teaspoon mace
2	cups sifted cake flour

Put sugar and eggs into a heavy saucepan. Stir over low heat until lukewarm. Do not let mixture get too hot. Remove from fire. Add the orange juice and water. Beat until cool, about 15 minutes. Mixture will be light and thick. Add the orange rind, extract and mace. Fold in flour gently. Pour into a greased and floured 10" x 15" pan (or 2 9-inch layer pans). Bake in a preheated 325° oven for 30-45 minutes or until a toothpick comes out cleanly when inserted into middle of cake. Do not overbake. Cake is traditionally served at teatime.

• • • • • • • • • • • • • • • • • •

Maple Glazed Carrots

8	medium carrots
1/2	cup pure maple syrup
3	tablespoons butter
1/4	teaspoon ground ginger

Peel carrots and cut into 1/2-inch thick slices. Cook in boiling water until tender. Drain well. Add the maple syrup and butter. Simmer until carrots are glazed with the sauce.

• • • • • • • • • • • • • • • • • •

Scallops Wrapped in Bacon

2	pounds scallops, drained
1	pound thin-sliced bacon (cut in half)

Wrap a piece of bacon around each scallop and secure with a toothpick. Place on a baking sheet and broil for about 10 minutes per side or until bacon is fully cooked. Watch carefully, lowering pan so scallops don't cook too quickly and burn. Serve warm. Serves 6-8.

| 2 | 6-ounce filet mignon steaks |
| 2 | tablespoons butter |

Season the steaks with salt and pepper. Heat a heavy skillet until very hot. Add the butter and add the steaks. Sauté about 7 minutes a side until desired doneness. Remove and set aside. Meanwhile make the blue cheese butter.

Blue Cheese Butter:

| 1/4 | cup butter, room temperature |
| 3 | tablespoons premium soft blue cheese |

Blend together well. Set aside.

Pan Sauce:

2	tablespoons butter
1	tablespoon minced shallots
1/2	cup minced fresh mushrooms
1/2	cup dry red wine
1/2	cup beef broth

After steaks are cooked and set aside, heat butter in same skillet. Sauté the shallots and mushrooms about 3 minutes. Remove pan and add the red wine. Return to heat and let wine reduce slightly. Add the broth and reduce sauce by 1/2, about 15 minutes. Season with salt and pepper.

On serving plate put 2-3 tablespoons sauce and top with the steak. Place 1 tablespoon blue cheese butter on top of steak. Serve immediately. Serves 2.

Filet Mignon
with Blue Cheese Butter

CONNECTICUT *The Constitution State*

Several Indian tribes lived in the area that is now Connecticut, foremost among them the Pequot and the Mohegan tribes. The first English settlement was founded in Windsor in 1633. Many other early settlements, including Hartford, were established and the colony expanded. Farming was the primary occupation until the 1800s when Eli Whitney's inventions and mass production methods moved Connecticut into an industrial boom. Many immigrants of different European countries flowed into the state to work in the factories. Connecticut is still an important industrial state as well as a favorite vacation destination. The insurance industry dominates Hartford and Bridgeport is home to commercial helicopter, jet engines and propeller production.

Like other New England states, Connecticut's cuisine stemmed from home-grown berries, vegetables and fruit trees. Nearly all land was farmed until the mid 19th century when agriculture began to decline. Fishing was always important. Shad fish in the Connecticut River and shell fish on the coast provide ample bounty for fine eating.

Early period foods included pies, cakes, soups, chowder, baked beans, roasted meats, breads and pork as well as dishes using "Indian" maize. Hartford is associated with the popularization of the "Election Cake", a large, enriched yeast cake, similar to modern coffee cakes or Hot Cross Buns.

Hartford Skyline, Connecticut.

Wild Mushroom Soup

2	tablespoons butter
1/4	cup shallot, minced
1/4	pound shiitake mushrooms
1/4	pound oyster mushrooms
1/4	pound portobello mushrooms
1	tablespoon fresh thyme, minced
1	clove garlic, minced
6	cups chicken stock

2	cups potatoes, cut in 2" pieces
1/4	cup Madeira wine
	Salt and pepper
1/2	cup fresh parsley, chopped
1/2	cup heavy cream

Melt butter in large heavy stock pot over medium high heat. Add shallots and sauté 1 minute. Add mushrooms and sauté 5 minutes. Add thyme and garlic and sauté 8 minutes. Stir in chicken stock and potatoes. Bring to boil. Reduce heat, cover and simmer for 25 minutes. Working in batches, puree soup in blender. Return soup to pot and add the Madeira. Season with salt and pepper. Stir in cream. Sprinkle with parsley and serve. Serves 6.

Yankee Doodle Noodle Salad

12	ounces ziti macaroni, cooked (about 4 1/4 cups)
2	1-ounce packages turkey jerky, cut into small bite-size pieces
1	large red onion, thinly sliced
1	large bunch red radishes, trimmed and sliced
1	cup fresh corn kernels, blanched or 1 can kernel corn, drained
2/3	cup Ranch style dressing
1/2	7-ounce package puffed cheese snacks (about 1 1/2 cups)
1/2	6-ounce package sour cream and onion-flavored potato chips (or BBQ) flavor, slightly crushed
1	cup cherry tomatoes, halved

Toss together cooked macaroni, turkey jerky, onion, radishes and corn. Mix with 1/2 cup of the ranch dressing. Fold in puffed cheese snacks. Scoop into an attractive salad bowl or into individual salad bowls. Drizzle with remaining ranch dressing. Top with potato chips. Garnish with a ring of cherry tomatoes. Serves 6-8.

Buttermilk Biscuits

4	cups all-purpose flour
2	teaspoons salt
1	tablespoon baking powder
2	teaspoons baking soda
1	cup cold vegetable shortening, cut into small pieces
1 1/2-2	cups buttermilk

Preheat oven to 375°. Sift together the flour, salt, baking powder, and baking soda. Cut in the shortening until mixture resembles coarse crumbs. Make a well in center and add 1 cup buttermilk. Using your hands gently fold the dry ingredients into the buttermilk until a sticky dough forms. Add more buttermilk if needed. Do not overwork. Turn out dough onto floured board. Gently knead, folding dough over itself 3-4 times (this creates layers). Press dough out to 1 to 1 1/2 inches thick. Cut with a 3-inch cookie cutter or cut into squares and lay on an ungreased cookie sheet. Brush the tops with the buttermilk or melted butter. Bake for 15-20 minutes or until golden brown. Makes 12-15 biscuits. Serve hot with butter, honey or jam.

Clam Fritters

1	pint freshly shucked clams, chopped
2	eggs
1/3	cup milk
1 1/2	cups flour
2	teaspoons baking powder
	Salt and pepper to taste

Beat eggs until light and fluffy. Add milk and stir in flour, baking powder, seasonings and clams. Drop by teaspoonfuls in hot fat (375 degrees. Dip spoon in hot oil before using. Fry the fritters until browned on outside, 3-5 minutes. Drain on paper toweling. Serves 6.

Corn Pudding

4	tablespoons unsalted butter
1	medium onion, chopped
3	tablespoons flour
2	eggs
3	cups frozen corn kernels (about 28 ounces), thawed
1	cup milk
1/2	teaspoons salt
1/4	teaspoon pepper

Position rack in center of oven and preheat to 350°F. Butter a 6-cup soufflé dish. Set aside. Melt butter in heavy large skillet over medium heat. Add onions and sauté until very soft, about 12 minutes. Mix in flour and stir 4 minutes. Transfer to bowl and cool to lukewarm. Add eggs to onion mixture and whisk to blend. Mix in corn, milk and salt. Season with pepper. Pour batter into prepared dish. Bake pudding until knife inserted into center comes out clean, about 1 hour. Serves 6.

Roasted Root Vegetables

3	medium carrots, cut into 1 1/2-inch pieces
3	cups small Red Bliss potatoes
3	medium parsnips, cut into 1 1/2-inch pieces
1	cup sweet potatoes cut into 1-inch cubes
1	large onion, cut into wedges
1/2	cup olive oil
1	tablespoon chopped fresh rosemary
2	teaspoons dried oregano
1	tablespoon chopped fresh thyme
1	teaspoon salt
1/2	teaspoon pepper

Place the cut-up vegetables in a large bowl. Add the oil and seasonings. Toss to cover all vegetables with the oil and seasonings. Spread out onto a large rimmed cookie sheet. Bake in a preheated 400° oven for 35-45 minutes. Serves 6-8.

ELECTION CAKE

This cake was used to feed government representatives who gathered in Hartford following state elections to count the ballots. Representatives stayed in local homes and housewives planned well in advance to prepare cakes that would keep.

Some food historians believe that this recipe from 1796 is the first recipe for Election Cake.

"Thirty quarts of flour, 10 pounds butter, 14 pounds sugar, 12 pounds raisins, 3 dozen eggs, one pint wine, one quart brandy, 4 ounces cinnamon, 4 ounces fine colander seed, 3 ounces ground allspice. Wet flour with milk to the consistency of bread overnight, adding one quart yeast. The next morning, work the butter and sugar together for half an hour, which will render the cake much lighter and whiter; when it has risen light work in every other ingredient except the plums (raisins), which work in when going into the oven." .....American Cookery, Amelia Simmons [Applewood Books:Bedford MA] 1996 (p. 43-44).

1771 - These cakes were baked to celebrate Election Days at least as early as 1771 in Connecticut, before the American Revolution of 1775. The Election Cake, as all cakes baked in colonial homes, was yeast-leavened, as there was no commercial baking powder, and they were baked in brick fireplace ovens. Colonial women vied with each other as to who baked the best cakes as families exchanged visits and treated their guest with slices of this cake. Historians feel that the recipe for Election Cake was adapted from popular period English yeast breads.

1830 - The cake became known as Hartford Election Cake when politicians there served it to men who voted a straight party ticket. While waiting for election results, it was a New England tradition to serve these huge Election Cakes (each cake weighing approximately 12 pounds). Housewives established their reputations as socialites and hostesses on the quality of their cakes.

Connecticut historian, J. Hammond Trumbell, in1886 wrote about it this way: "Election Day (the first Thursday in May), the reddest letter in our calendar, brightened the whole year. Good housekeepers were expected to have finished their spring cleaning long before... 'lection cake was rising to make ready for the oven: and few homes were too poor to offer these refreshments to visitors."

2	cups whole milk, scalded
1/2	cup light brown sugar, tightly packed
1/2	teaspoon salt
21/4	teaspoons dry yeast
5	cups flour, sifted
11/2	cups sugar
3/4	cup unsalted butter (or 1/2 cup unsalted butter and
1/4	cup vegetable shortening)
2	eggs
11/2	cups raisins or currants
1/4	pound citron, sliced thin (optional)
1/2	teaspoon nutmeg
1/2	teaspoon mace

Combine milk, brown sugar and salt in a mixing bowl. When lukewarm, add yeast and 4 1/2 cups of the flour. Knead thoroughly. Place in a lightly greased bowl, turning once to coat the dough. Cover and let rise for 2 to 3 hours in a warm place, until double in bulk.

Punch the dough down. Cream the sugar and shortening, and add to the dough. Stir in the eggs, raisins, citron, nutmeg, mace and remaining 1/2 cup flour. Mix thoroughly by hand or in a heavy-duty mixer, using a dough hook. Place in two greased 5" x 9" bread pans. Cover and let rise again until double in bulk. Bake in a preheated, moderate oven (350 degrees) until brown, about 45 minutes. Cool on wire racks 10 minutes before removing from pans. Makes 2 loaves.

Icing:

1	cup sugar
1/3	cup water
1/4	teaspoon cream of tartar or 1/2 teaspoon light corn syrup
	Dash of salt
2	egg whites
1	teaspoon vanilla

Put sugar, water, cream of tartar or corn syrup, and salt in a saucepan and bring to a boil. Stir until the sugar dissolves. Cool slightly. Add this syrup in a slow stream to egg whites, beating constantly. Add vanilla and continue beating until soft peaks form. This icing can be used immediately or refrigerated for several hours.

• •

APPLE BUTTER

This apple butter is cooked in the oven and is easier than using a stock pot as the oven method requires very little stirring whereas the pot method requires almost constant stirring. Also, the flavor is intensified in the slow-cooking oven method.

2	quarts water
1	tablespoon salt
6	pounds apples, cored, peeled and sliced
2	quarts sweet cider
4	cups sugar
1	teaspoon ground cinnamon
1/2	teaspoon ground cloves
1/2	teaspoon ground allspice

Preheat oven to 350 degrees. Combine water and salt. Add apples. Drain well but do not rinse slices. Put through the food processor (or food grinder using finest blade). Measure pulp and juice. There should be about 2 quarts. Combine mixture with cider and place in a large oven-proof pot or Dutch oven. Put in the middle of the oven and simmer for 3 to 3-1/2 hours until thick and cooked down to about half. Stir every half hour. Put mixture through a sieve or food mill; it should yield about 2-1/4 quarts. Combine sugar and spices; add to sauce and return to oven. Continue simmering about 1-1/2 hours, stirring every half hour, until thick. To test for doneness, spoon a small amount onto a cold plate. If no liquid oozes around the edges, the apple butter is cooked. Pour into hot sterilized jars and seal. Makes 2 quarts or about 10 six-ounce glasses.

Best Ever

2	cups flour
3	tablespoons sugar
2	teaspoons. baking powder
1/2	teaspoon. salt
1/2	teaspoon baking soda
1 1/2	cups. buttermilk
3	tablespoons. melted butter
1	beaten egg

In a medium bowl, mix the dry ingredients. In a large bowl, mix the liquid ingredients. Slowly mix the dry ingredients into the liquid ingredients. Pour 1/2 to 1/4 cup portions onto a frying pan and cook. To make blueberry pancakes, add 1 cup of fresh blueberries.

Pancakes

INDEX